· The Bio-Imagery Method of ·
Breast Enlargement
& Waist Reduction

The Story of a Revolutionary New Figure Development Program and the Women Who Have Used It

•The Bio-Imagery Method of•
Breast Enlargement & Waist Reduction

The Story of a Revolutionary New Figure Development Program and the Women Who Have Used It

by Craig Stratton, B.A., M.A.

Published by Ad-Images
Grand Rapids, Michigan

AD-IMAGES
PUBLISHING
Waters Building
Grand Rapids, Michigan 49503

First Printing - February 1982
Second Printing - March 1982
Third Printing - April 1982
Fourth Printing - July 1982
Fifth Printing - November 1982
Sixth Printing - August 1983

Acknowledgement is made for permission to reprint the following:

New Dimensions ®II   Bio-Imagery Programming ™ Script One — The Basic Program © 1978 and 1982 by New Directions, Inc.

New Dimensions ®II   Bio-Imagery Programming ™ Script Two — The Accelerated Program © 1982 by New Directions, Inc.

Breakthrough™ Bio-Imagery Programming™ — A Maximum Effect Program © 1982 by New Directions, Inc.

The terms New Dimensions, Bio-Imagery, Bio-Image, and Bio-Imagery Programming are trademarks of New Directions, Inc., Suite 208, Dept. BK 200, 161 Ottawa N.W., Grand Rapids, Michigan 49503.

ISBN 0-943154-00-6

CONTENTS

CONTENTS

PART III
UNDERSTANDING
BIO-IMAGERY PROGRAMMING:
WHAT IT IS AND HOW IT WORKS

PART V
IMPROVING THE EFFECTIVENESS
OF THE PROGRAM:
HOW TO ACHIEVE MAXIMUM RESULTS

PART VI
YOUR RESOURCE GUIDE:
QUESTIONS AND ANSWERS ABOUT
THE PROGRAM

RESEARCH AND STUDY GUIDE

• The Bio-Imagery Method of •
Breast Enlargement & Waist Reduction

The Story of a Revolutionary New Figure Development Program and the Women Who Have Used It

A Revolutionary New Way To Have Larger Breasts And A Lovelier Figure

Recent independent clinical studies by research scientists and medical doctors reported in recognized scientific journals have demonstrated an amazing fact: significant breast enlargement can be achieved without surgery, exercise, or special diet. The studies produced outstanding test results like these: *all women participating in the studies achieved measurable increases in actual breast size; average increases of total breast size were approximately two inches with increases ranging as high as 3.54 inches;* increases were of actual breast size, not just the size of the chest or chest muscles. In addition, other benefits were reported in the studies: increased fullness and firmness of the breasts; more attractive proportioning of the breasts; spontaneous weight loss; smaller waistline; and, other positive changes such as increased self-esteem and self-confidence.

If you have ever thought that you would like to have larger, firmer, fuller breasts you owe it to yourself to learn about this new method.

There's something very special about knowing that you look ... and feel your very best. There's a special magic in moving easily, gracefully ... in looking great in the clothes you wear. In the pages that follow, you will have an opportunity to explore the exciting new evidence for a new, simple method to help you achieve your personal figure development goals.

Here you will learn about the method and how it works. To enjoy maximum benefits from the Program it's helpful first to understand its basic principles. And it's important to take the time to review these principles to assure yourself of pleasure and success as you are progressing toward your own personal figure development goals. This exciting new Program is designed to teach you how to reach your goal for having an attractive figure, through a simple learning procedure that you can use in the privacy of your own home, in just a few minutes a day.

The Program can be used with complete confidence since it is a totally *natural* method of learning to improve your figure with *normal* bodily processes and *normal* psychological processes. It maximizes your potential for change and improvement. Because it is a completely natural method it is not only totally safe, but it is highly effective.

The Program has been prepared in consultation with an internationally known clinical psychologist and is based on extensive clinical studies utilizing fundamental learning processes and specific clinical studies which evaluated the effects of such processes on breast enlargement. Thus, its principles and procedures for helping people learn to reach their figure development goals are well-tested and corroborated.

This book cites the evidence for the method, explains how it works, and shows you in simple, step-by-step instructions how you can learn to use it effectively in your own home.

While the book has been designed expressly to help women learn the method on their own, it may also be of interest to professionals seeking a comprehensive summary of the research data, or a useful handbook that they can suggest to women who wish to learn the method.

PART I

Your Guide To Using This Book

1

An Overview: How To Get The Most Out Of This Book

From Australia to Puerto Rico — from London to Japan — from Boston to Burbank — a quiet revolution is taking place. Women everywhere are discovering that now there *is* a new way to have larger, lovelier breasts, a smaller waistline, and a more attractive figure . . . without exercise, surgery, diets or drugs. In all of the 50 states — and across the globe — a runaway bestselling breast enlargement program is helping women to reach their own personal figure development goals . . . to enjoy lovelier figures . . . and to develop the increased poise and self-confidence that only an enhanced self-image can bring.

For years women have had two choices for breast enlargement: surgery, or highly advertised gimmicks — one, an expensive, complicated, and sometimes risky procedure; the other, a sure road to disappointment.

Now a new discovery has marched out of the science labs and into the privacy of women's homes. For the first time there's a method that's so simple, so natural, so safe, that women can use it at home ... and can enjoy the benefits of lovelier figures easily and effectively. For the first time there's a new proven method that's based on documented scientific evidence.

YOUR INTRODUCTION TO A
NEW BREAST ENLARGEMENT PROGRAM

Here is the story of this new breast enlargement discovery ... and the story of the women who have used it. Here is the first truly practical guide to show *you*, step-by-step, how you can learn this new method. From a comprehensive survey of the scientific data on which the Program is based, to the easy-to-follow instructions for using it, this book takes you on an exciting journey that can lead you to the lovelier, more attractive figure that you've always dreamed of.

This is the story of the *New Dimensions Figure Enhancement System.* This Program — designed in consultation with an internationally known clinical scientist — utilizes a process known as *Bio-Imagery Programming.* Here you will learn precisely what it is, how it was developed, and how it works. Here you will read the comments, and follow the day-to-day progress, of dozens of women who have used the Program. Here you will find a truly complete and practical guide to help *you* to learn the method for yourself — in a rapid, easy, and enjoyable fashion. This chapter provides a road map for a successful trip for you on your personal journey to a lovelier figure.

It includes a guide for the use of the book, the comments of women who have used the Program, and helpful suggestions to enable you to begin it as quickly as possible.

HOW YOU CAN LEARN THE PROGRAM: YOUR GUIDE TO THE USE OF THIS BOOK

And now it's time to begin your journey. First, here is an overview that will serve as your guide to the use of this book.

In Part II, *New Discoveries About Breast Enlargement,* you will be introduced to the scientific data on which the Program is based. Part II discusses the role of blood circulation in breast growth, and how improving circulation in the breast area results in increased breast size. It analyzes the latest research on breast enlargement and examines the clinical studies which led to the development of the Program. You'll find out about the specific results of the studies, and the many benefits enjoyed by the women who participated in them. Their experiences can help you to understand the marvelous potential of the Program and the kind of results it can produce.

Part III, *Understanding Bio-Imagery Programming: What It Is And How It Works,* explores the *Bio-Imagery Programming* method itself. Here you'll discover how it's designed, what it consists of, and how it works. Here you will learn how thousands of people in the last decade have learned simple, relaxing methods of improving circulation in various parts of the body. Here you will be introduced to the ways in which these methods have been applied to help enlarge the breasts, naturally and safely. The information in Part III will help you gain a better understanding of the method, and help you to enhance the effectiveness of your own personal Program.

Part IV, *How To Use The Program: A Step-By-Step Guide,* is the "how-to-do-it" section. Here is your manual of instructions for the Program itself. It includes a helpful Progress Chart to enable you to keep track of your results as you progress toward your goal.

In Part V, *Improving The Effectiveness Of The Program: How To Achieve Maximum Results,* you'll find two full chapters containing actual Progress Charts of women who have used the Program. You can compare your day-to-day progress with women of literally every shape, size, and description. Part V also includes a special supplementary Program to help you to get off to a fast start, overcome plateaus, and maximize your results.

Part VI, *Your Resource Guide: Questions And Answers About The New Dimensions Program,* provides a comprehensive question and answer section to give you all of the facts you need to insure your success. It is followed by a special Reading and Study Guide for those who wish to learn more about the scientific data on which the Program is based.

Each of these sections of the book plays an important part in your success on your journey. But it's your final destination . . . your goal . . . the actual achievement of a lovelier figure which is the most important thing to you. You'll find it helpful to know before you begin what kind of results can be achieved with the Program. And nowhere is that story told as eloquently as it is by the women who have actually used it.

WHAT WOMEN ARE SAYING
ABOUT THE PROGRAM

Here are samples of the comments of women who have used the *New Dimensions* Program*. Follow their personal stories as they travel the roads that took them from skepticism to success. Examine their concerns and their problems; their progress and their enthusiasm for their lovelier figures and enhanced self-images. Here, in their personal stories, you will learn the true potential of the Program. Here you will see what can be achieved by deciding to follow the easy steps outlined in this book:

*"I have more confidence in myself than I ever had
... it is fantastic." (Bust increase 2", waist decrease 3½")*

V.S., Kansas City, MO

"32A to 36C, I am very pleased!"

S.J., Longview, WA

*The original signed copy of the comments made by each of these women is on file at New Directions, Inc. To protect the privacy of the women involved no names are shown for any of the quotations or for any of the charts reproduced in this book.

It is important to note that, although occasional reference is made in these letters to the use of recordings, those references are to an earlier version of the Program. The entire Program is now in *written* form and is contained in the pages of this book. This newly improved Program has been greatly revised and expanded and incorporates significant improvements based on extensive experience with the Program, as well as the latest research findings on the method.

The book itself is designed so that it can be used totally independently of any recordings. However, Talking Book Transcripts of portions of the book are available for those who prefer this convenience. (See chapter 7 for a discussion of ways to use the Program.) No medical claims of any sort are made for the recordings.

". . . my bust measurement went to 38½. Needless to say I was pleased with the results . . . Before writing this letter, I remeasured my bust to see if I had lost any that I gained from your program and I was so pleased to see the tape measure reach to 38½ again."

Yours truly,
A pleased customer, Raleigh, SC

"I'm very pleased and much larger . . . this plan is fantastic. I've told friends who wanted to hear and friends who didn't . . . I never had much for breasts . . . now they're a 38. It takes some getting used to 'cause they don't fit where the others did."

S.M., Pontiac, MI

"I am a mother of two children. After I breast fed them the firmness of my breasts had disappeared. I tried a number of other products that promised good results. After many hours of dedication I found my efforts were in vain. I was about to give up when I read your advertisement. I thought it sounded like something different, so I decided to give it one <u>last</u> try. I'm very glad I tried your system. It's effortless and relaxing. With two children I was always glad to 'get away' and take time to follow your program. I received immediate results and improvements thereafter. I was actually quite surprised with the results. I not only received the firmness I was after, but I was pleased to find an extra bonus, added inches (3" bust increase). I am very pleased and satisfied with your system. I'd recommend it above all other products intending

the same promised results. I will continue using it when I feel the need."

S.G., Regina, Sask.

". . . Bio-Imagery really added 3 whole inches to my bust. I was fascinated with the results and still am."

Thank you.
L.C., Baltimore, MD
(3" bust increase, 2" waist reduction.)

"I began noticing a difference very soon after I started the program (within weeks) and now the difference is clearly seen (from 34A to 36B-C). My husband as well as I myself are grateful to you."

D.S., Salt Lake City, UT

"At first I was very doubtful of the possibilities. I have tried a lot of different exercise equipment and protein to increase my bustline. But nothing worked for me . . . Even losing the few extra pounds was hard, so I figured on giving the record a try. And after 5 weeks I stopped doubting. I saw good results, and better, then great results. All I can say is I am definitely pleased with the results. I love the new me. I would highly recommend this product to anyone and everyone who wants to be the best they can be. Thank you for such a great product and what the record has done for me."

Thanks again.
L.R., Syracuse, NY
(4" bust increase, 3" waist decrease,
12 pound weight reduction.)

"I never thought something like this would work. I'm getting married in May and I wanted to look the best I could. And with this program I do! It makes your breasts full and sturdy. Your waist automatically feels smaller every time you listen to the tape. It's also great for just relaxing and relieving stress. My bust was not in proportion with the rest of my body. Now . . . I weigh 109 and I measure 34C-24-34 — perfect proportions for my small frame. And talk about curves! Raquel Welch eat your heart out. Thanks for a wonderful program! I will still continue the program."

S.S., Laredo, TX

". . . I had used several methods before and nothing had worked. I have had 3 children, and I am so very pleased with the results I have had. (4½" bust increase, 3" waist decrease, 5 pound weight loss.) I will recommend it to anyone who asks about it. Thank you very much."

K.T., Salt Lake City, UT

"At 26 I had given up hope for a growth spurt . . . I decided to give your program a try. I started in February, but decided to only measure myself at the end of each 5-week period because I discourage easily. I am very pleased with the results and have recommended it to several friends. My ribs did protrude. My breast bone is no longer visable. I went from a 32A to a 34C. I have every confidence in achieving my goal. I have gained another ½ inch since the 16th week."

C.S., Miamisburg, OH

An Overview: How To Get The Most Out Of This Book

"Before I discovered the program I never gave much thought to my figure as a woman, but I had tried to lose weight, 25 lbs. in all. Unfortunately I lost everything else and also this really made me feel inadequate! I knew I could do it if only I had the stamina and procedure to build myself up in the right way. So that's when the program came in. At first I responded very slowly until I learned the process and now after 3 weeks after the end I am gaining about an inch a month (3½" bust increase; 2½" waist decrease) . . . I wrote down the steps on paper so I can concentrate better when I'm at work all day. I know the mind can bring about almost any kind of change and I'm glad it was finally realized for breast development! Very important!"
C.C., Salt Lake City, UT

". . . I just wanted you to know that I have completed the program and you were quite right. I don't know how you could do it but I actually got inches coming in so quickly. Before you know it there it is, beautiful and firm. I actually lost a few inches from my waist. Now you have my opinion on your product and I truly hope that your other customers will tell you all the same results."
Frances L.

"Although I was only able to play the record once (my record player broke!) I already had some knowledge of meditating and visioning, so I was able to do the programming on my own once I grasped the idea. I do not have trouble with my weight, so my waist measurements and weight are the same. However, each breast has enlarged at

least 2½" and I am absolutely delighted. Also, the meditation is very therapeutic and it is so very relaxing and refreshing. I plan to go as far as I can with this program."

Thank you!
A very sincerely satisfied customer!
L.D., Arlington, TX

"I can't believe it was possible to just give me a little more fullness, where I needed it. It's true about how people see you, when you become a little more endowed. I only wish I could lose a little more weight. That part is so stubborn to shed. I've noticed quite a difference in my waist, and it gives me a good feeling. Bio-Imagery really works and I'm glad I didn't have to depend on pills, etc."

M.R., Onset, MA

". . . I highly recommend your program . . . Your program gave a new 'spring' into my life . . . wonderful at relaxing after a hectic day at work and that is an extra that my life was without."

Thank you,
Marlene

". . . Besides the gain in the bust, I lost weight and 1½ inches off my waist. I am continuing to use the program now with the anticipation of getting closer to my goals. I also use the program for the sheer relaxation and revitalization with which it provides me."

Thank you.
G.R., Reading, PA

"The program really did the job on my breasts. It seemed to have gotten to work the first time I tried it. My relaxation was terrific. I did not move a single muscle at all. I went from a 32" size breast to a 40 size, and now I'm satisfied. My fiance gives me more attention now. Thanks a million."

R.V., Philadelphia, PA

"Filled bustline, toned muscles. Took away extra inches around waist. Gave me time each day to totally relax. Lost a total of 11 pounds. I feel better every day, especially in the mornings. I'm not as tired as I used to be. I have and will continue to recommend this to friends."

S.H., Cocoa, FL

". . . I am so pleased with your program and what is happening to me. Thank you."

J.H., Indianapolis, IN

"I am a dancer and anything that helps my self-image helps my dance — both the program and the physical changes did that!"

*C.R., Orofino, ID
(2½" bust increase, 1½"
waist decrease.)*

". . . I am pleased, because at first I really doubted it could work. The proof, however, is in my measurements!"

*Thanks.
F.V., Elmhurst, NY*

". . . very happy with the results . . . a very good program and a very safe and inexpensive program."
L.H., Lancaster, OH

"My boyfriend sure was surprised."
P.P., Nacogdoches, TX

"It helped me reach certain goals that I had before, but had no hope until I used your product."
A.T., Cincinnati, OH
(3" bust increase, 2" waist decrease, 5 pound weight reduction.)

". . . It has helped me to increase my bust size at least by one cup . . . It has also helped me lose weight that I couldn't lose before and my waist size is finally down to where I want it. Also, I've been able to stay more relaxed throughout the days."
W.M., Paust, RI

". . . What I guess amazed me was I went on more or less a fast at the same time I started my program. And, instead of losing more of my top I gained and I feel pretty."
S.O., Minneapolis, MN

"I would recommend your product to anyone because I got great results . . . I enjoyed it and I feel better about myself . . . And it really works. When I first started the program I asked myself how can that do anything. I thought I had wasted your time and mine. But I said what could I lose by trying it for a few weeks. I'm glad I did. Thank

you for the program. P.S. I could go on and on."

Sincerely,
Mrs. B.

". . . Before starting the program my bust size was a 33½. After the first week I gained a half inch; though I played the recording 15 times. In my eagerness to achieve fast results each week preceeding, the recording was played up to 10 times. By the fourth week my bust size became a 35 . . . I can say very honestly I was happy with the program and the results it promised. I learned to relax and enjoyed the comfort the recording brought."

S.V., Mt. Sinai, NY

"I followed your program exactly. However, I did not keep a statistical chart of before and after inches. I did not care about inches. My only goal was to be able to see an increase in size and I have! Thanks for your effective, natural system.

D.

"My wife received a copy of your New Dimensions program recently; in good time too, considering mail service from here to Michigan and back. She has tried a good sampling of the available market in Bust Expanders over the last five years, and none have done much more than beef up her shoulder muscles . . . Still, through all of her life, having been what I would call a 'late bloomer', she has never been quite sure of what she was trying to achieve — inside, in terms of her own awareness of her feminine self. In my opinion, your program has

23

hit the nail on the head ... I am quite sure that what we are observing here is ... psychology emerging into a practical science, applied for the benefit of all in solving a common problem ... <u>Improvements — overall — are obvious.</u> Self-confidence (as a direct result of observable success, and of the program's efforts in that direction too), posture, and of course the increase in observed size are all immediate results. I do not believe that I am being over zealous, but am confident that your program has tied together all of the normal social effects which may be commonplace for some women in their adolescence, forming a healthy attitude about themselves, but which I know was lacking in my wife's background. She does not know I am writing this — it is important, I think, that she know that she is crossing this river on her own, in her own mind, in her own way. I have tried my best to help, admire, and encourage her, and even set up a special system for her to listen to the program in bed every evening. I am sure that the improvements have just begun ... I am really fascinated to know how a person put together such an incredibly powerful tool ... Well, for what it's worth, thank you. I don't really intend for this letter to be a testimonial on the whole, but it certainly helps put a check mark on the wall for one that worked ... A questionably-motivated person ... is charging $250.00 for a program which, I have a feeling, is identical, or nearly so, to the New Dimensions Program ... We looked into that program, but shied away, for obvious reasons ... Well, in any case, I wish you much deserved success. I am certainly appreciative of what you are *doing — or rather what your program is doing — for my wife."*

> *Thanks*
> *R.W., Sacramento, CA*
> *(R.W.'s wife gained 3" in her bust*
> *and lost 2" in her waist.)*

The message rings clear in letter after letter ... increased breast sizes, smaller waistlines, loss of excess pounds ... and, equally important, a new sense of pride emanating from a better, more vital, self-image.

HOW YOU CAN BEGIN AT ONCE: A PLAN FOR USING THE PROGRAM WHILE YOU READ THE BOOK

Most people like to start a project quickly — without fully understanding how it works. We suggest that you take a little time first to understand fully how this Program works. After all, if you tried to cook a new dish before knowing what ingredients to use, how to mix them, and how to prepare them, you might not succeed too well. This book is designed to help you understand, in depth, how this method works.

If you are curious about the Program itself — the specific methods and techniques, as well as the instructions on how to use them — you might like to read Part IV first (chapters 7, 8, 9 and 10). This will give you a "feel" for the method and help you to appreciate its simplicity. And if you just can't resist the urge to start on your Program, so that it can begin working for you while you are reading the balance of this book, you will find that the instructions, and the method, are so simple that you can get a head start on the Program in this way. These few chapters will show you how.

But don't stop there. If you are really serious about gaining the tremendous advantages of this Program, and wish to insure your success, read this entire book. You'll find it informative and interesting. *Knowing more about the method helps to make it more effective.* You may wish to dip into the reference section, at the end of this book, and read some of the material that appeals to you.

Follow the simple, relaxing, and helpful procedures — as you learn by doing. The more you practice these procedures, the more beneficial the results are likely to be. Practice does make perfect!

And so, we wish you a pleasant, stimulating, and successful journey on your path toward breast enlargement and figure enhancement.

BON VOYAGE!

PART II

New Discoveries About Breast Enlargement

2

Newly Discovered Facts About Breast Enlargement

Next time you're shopping in a crowded store watch the women around you as they search for just the right things that will help them look their very best. They know that their appearance helps determine their success and happiness in life. They know that how they look affects how they feel about themselves . . . and how others feel about them.

But somehow, some women seem to have an advantage. They just naturally have attractive well-proportioned figures that let them shop easily and look sensational in the clothes they wear.

But what about the others — the thousands of women who would like to have better figures — to be more attractive — to enjoy the poise and confidence that comes with knowing that they look their very best?

In the quest for a lovelier figure millions of dollars have

been spent. And *until now,* the results have been largely disappointing. Padded bras are a poor substitute for a *naturally good figure.* The bust exercisers have been proven ineffective in increasing breast size. The protein and enzyme supplements simply fatten the whole body. Even the women who have breast enlargement surgery face the disadvantages of scarring, the possibility of unnatural looking results, and the dangers of the anesthetics and possible infections. And yet, the quest goes on . . . in search of a safe, effective, natural way to enlarge the breasts and enhance the figure.

NEW RESEARCH
ON BREAST ENLARGEMENT

It seems incredible, in this modern day and age, with all of the great advances our society has known . . . with all of its technological achievements, that scientists have not discovered a new breast enlargement method.

Well, here is some startling news.

The fact is that such a discovery has recently been made. The fact is that now new clinical research has demonstrated the effectiveness of a revolutionary new breast enlargement method.

In the words of an internationally known clinical scientist:

"Recent independent clinical tests conducted by research scientists and medical doctors and reported in recognized scientific journals, provide documented evidence for a totally new breast enlargement technique. * It's a method that works in a totally safe and natural way — without surgery,

---

*Specific details about these studies, the scientists who conducted them, and the journals they appeared in can be found in chapters 3 and 4 and in the Reading and Study Guide.

exercise, or special diets or drugs. It's a simple, pleasant technique that women can use in the privacy of their own homes, in just a few minutes a day, while they're relaxing. Best of all it's a method that really works."

But what exactly is this new method? And how does it work? When and how was it discovered and why don't more people know about it?

The answer to these questions can be found in the following true story which demonstrates the amazing physiology of the human body and its remarkable ability to adapt and respond to unique circumstances.*

One cold winter night an 18 year old college student was driving on an ice covered road in Jackson, Michigan. Suddenly he lost control of his car. He skidded and plunged into an ice covered pond. He struggled, inhaled water, and lost consciousness.

Thirty-eight minutes later rescuers pulled the "lifeless" body out of the water. He was declared dead at the scene. Then a remarkable thing happened. While being loaded into the ambulance the supposedly lifeless body gasped. Startled rescuers immediately began revival efforts and a life was saved. Later this same young man pulled in "A" grades in college shattering age old myths about drowning and brain damage from lack of oxygen.

An extraordinary story. But how does it relate to breast enlargement? It relates in *two* very important ways. *First,* it demonstrates the vital importance of knowing *all* of the facts in any given situation. For example, scientists have now gathered extensive additional evidence to prove

*Cold Water Drowning – A New Lease on Life: U.S. Department of Transportation, Michigan Sea Grant Program, Advisory Service, MICHU-56-77-104, CG-513.

that many cold water drowning victims can survive even after being underwater amazing lengths of time. Although there have been active attempts to publicize this fact through newspaper publicity and even government pamphlets, tragically, researchers say that every year 3,000 more drowning victims are lost because of lack of information about this life-saving fact.

Similarly, it has been estimated that as many as 100,000 women will have breast enlargement surgery this year without ever knowing about the recent clinical evidence for a remarkable new, safe, natural way to enlarge the breasts without surgery.

Why? Because of lack of information — lack of knowledge. Every new scientific discovery faces this painfully slow process of becoming widely-known and accepted. With today's knowledge growing at such a phenomenal rate, it's physically impossible for scientists, doctors, and the public to keep up with the latest discoveries in every field. It often takes 5 to 10 years — and in many cases much longer — for new discoveries to become widely-known and utilized.

And that's the purpose of this book — to provide you with up-to-date information about the latest discoveries in the field of natural breast enlargement. You owe it to yourself to learn how this new method works and how it increases actual breast size.

This brings us to the *second* reason why the story about the young man who almost drowned relates to breast enlargement. It's a relationship that will probably surprise you. *The very same bodily mechanisms that saved the young man's life are the mechanisms that scientists now believe can help to increase breast size.*

Sound remarkable? Well it is. But, these methods have been tested and corroborated by research scientists and medical doctors through clinical studies that have been reported in highly respected scientific journals.

Let's examine the nature of the mechanisms that helped save this young man from drowning, as accurately as scientists understand them.

Time can be a very precious commodity. Certainly for the young man whose car sank beneath the ice covered pond, every second, every minute ticking away was a matter of life or death. Doctors knew he could only survive 3 or 4 minutes without oxygen. And yet, after the long interval of 38 minutes he did, incredibly, survive. Why? How?

The truth of the matter is that his vital organs – his heart, his lungs, his brain – continued to make use of the oxygen that was in his sytem. For his body did an amazing thing – it concentrated blood circulation in those vital areas.

These same astonishing mechanisms of the body normally are working continually – every second, every minute, every hour, day and night, to meet your body's needs.

These mechanisms are always monitoring and are always responding. Even as you are reading this, your normal bodily mechanisms are working right now. Is your body to cold? Too warm? Are you sitting uncomfortably and cutting off the circulation to an arm or a leg? The body automatically responds from moment to moment to correct the problem and provide just the right amount of blood circulation in each part of the body.

But these bodily mechanisms sometimes go awry. Sometimes they slow down or even "go to sleep."

THE ROLE OF BLOOD CIRCULATION
IN BREAST GROWTH

For a moment now, let's go back in time to the period in your life when your figure was just beginning to develop. The developmental stage in a young girl's life is a time of hectic physical, bio-chemical, and emotional changes. And the demands for increased blood circulation in the developing areas of the body is at a peak. For the breasts to grow and develop, proper blood circulation is vital. For it's the blood that brings the essential chemicals and nutrients that stimulate growth.

But again, the body selects and monitors. And if other demands of the body are more important, those needs may be favored, and the breasts may be neglected. Without the right combination of nutritional and bio-chemical factors the breasts may miss this unique opportunity to grow to their maximum potential.

For more than a decade scientists have been teaching people simple learning techniques for improving blood circulation to various parts of the body. These learning procedures are based on more than a decade of studies which demonstrate that individuals can *learn* to control blood flow, pulse rate, body temperature and many other body functions formerly believed beyond human control. The fascinating relationship between mind and body, studied for years by psychologists, played a significant role in the psychological research in these interrelated areas: learning theory; methods of inducing relaxation so as to induce more effective and harmonious general bodily processes; methods of insuring improvement in self-image and self-concept; psychological methods of learning feedback; methods of improved visualization and self-imagery;

and studies on the specific effects of many of these procedures. These studies demonstrated the effectiveness of appropriate learning procedures in improving general, normal physiological functioning and in re-establishing more natural, *balanced* bodily processes. These principles and methods have been time and research-tested.

THE EFFECTS OF IMPROVED BLOOD CIRCULATION ON BREAST ENLARGEMENT

Until recently, no one ever thought of applying these methods to the improvement of blood circulation to the breast area so that breast size could be increased even years after the normal developmental stage had passed. Then some teams of research scientists working independently, in different parts of the country, conducted a series of clinical studies that signaled a scientific breakthrough of monumental significance! Those studies provided clinical proof of an amazing fact: the fact that improving blood circulation to the breast area actually stimulated substantial increases in breast size in women of virtually any age.

Here is the evaluation of these studies as analyzed by an internationally-known clinical scientist who critically reviewed the scientific data for these methods:

"These studies demonstrate that women can increase actual breast size by improving blood circulation to the breast area with simple, and relaxing techniques. The studies demonstrated that consistent use of these methods produced outstanding test results like these: average increases in breast size of 2 inches . . . increases ranging as high as 3.54 inches . . . increases for all women in the

studies. The increases were of actual breast size and not just changes in back or chest muscles.

The techniques not only increased breast size, but were effective in increasing fullness and firmness of the breasts, reducing sagging, and in solving the problem of women who formerly had breasts of uneven sizes. Other benefits were reported in the studies: benefits like the reduction of bulgy waistlines — and a variety of positive effects in some other aspects of their lives."

These studies demonstrate persuasively that at last there *is* a revolutionary new breast enlargement method. A way to have larger, fuller, firmer breasts to help you look and feel great! Most women want to have stunning figures, but relatively few have them. Now there's a way to join that select group — a logical, sensible key to the figure you've always dreamed of.

Yes, time is a precious commodity. It can be our friend ... or our enemy. For. the young man whose life hung in the balance every additional moment was vital.

And for you, this moment in time is especially meaningful. For now *you* can learn the latest facts about breast enlargement. And time *is* on your side.

Now, *you* have the opportunity to benefit from the new discoveries. Now you can learn the Program for yourself and enjoy the benefits of a lovelier figure and an improved self-image. And maybe next time you're shopping in that crowded store, you can be in that select group of women with natural, attractive figures.

3

Current Research Findings For a New Breast Enlargement Method

To get the maximum benefit from this new breast enlargement method, it's helpful to be aware of the scientific data on which it is based. Here you will be introduced to the clinical studies which signaled the advent of this exciting scientific breakthrough.

Within recent years scientists have begun to explore some new fields of scientific endeavor. In the process remarkable discoveries have been made. For example, during the last decade clinical studies have demonstrated that an individual can actually learn to control blood pressure, heartbeat, and breathing rate — functions formerly believed to be beyond human control[1]. In the light

[1]For the specific references for these footnotes please see the chapter references at the end of each chapter. In addition, detailed publishing information for each reference can be found in the appropriate section of the comprehensive bibliography in the Reading and Study Guide at the back of the book.

of these new discoveries the power of the mind to control bodily functions has taken on a new meaning (see chapter 5).

NEW CLINICAL STUDIES ON
BREAST ENLARGEMENT

As a logical outgrowth of these discoveries independent researchers, working separately in different parts of the country, have recently been studying a new approach to breast enlargement: the integration of several different methods of stimulating dormant or inhibited physiological processes so as to increase breast size . . . without surgery, diet, or exercise. The concepts integrated in the research include: *Visual Imagery* — the remarkable ability of the human mind to affect behavioral changes through visual imagery; *Self-Suggestion* — the ability of the mind to affect bodily functions formerly thought to be entirely reflexive (clinical research studies had demonstrated that monitored self-suggestion can markedly influence many autonomic systems of the body).

The results of these studies of a totally new approach to breast enlargement were remarkably favorable. Highly significant improvements in breast size were achieved with a simple, safe, and reliable procedure. For the first time in recorded history breast enlargement had been achieved without surgical or medical procedures. The studies were conducted with appropriate controls and reported in recognized scientific journals. Measurements included vertical and horizontal dimensions as well as circumference. Unlike so-called bust developer exercisers marketed for many years, which at best affected only muscular development in the chest and back muscles and not actual breast size, this new scientific breakthrough in breast enlargement affected *actual breast size.*

When the first study was completed the results were exciting. *The AVERAGE increase in breast circumference of the participants was 2.11 inches!*[2] Additional studies confirmed that here at last was a simple, effective way to increase breast size. Moreover, further studies revealed additional benefits; increased fullness and firmness, better proportioning, smaller waistlines, etc.

Here at last was a vitally important scientific breakthrough in breast enlargement techniques; a sensible alternative to surgery; a technique, demonstrated in controlled scientific studies, with significant measurable results for virtually all participating women; a technique that can be utilized by any woman, in the privacy of her own home, in just a few minutes a day, while relaxing; a technique that can increase the actual size of the breasts, as well as firming and shaping them.

A SUMMARY OF THE
RESULTS OF THE CLINICAL STUDIES

In summary, these studies show that the following results can be achieved:

1. *All women* who participated in the specific research and clinical studies on breast enlargement reported in the scientific journals *achieved measurable increases in breast size.*

2. *Average increases of total breast size in two independent clinical studies were approximately two inches with increases ranging as high as 3.54 inches.*

3. *The increases were of actual breast size* not just the
size of the chest or chest muscles. Breast size was
measured both vertically and horizontally, as well
as in circumference, to verify that the *actual size* of
the breasts had increased.

4. Increased fullness and firmness of the breasts was
reported by *all* women participating in one of the
studies[3]. This was vitally important to those who
previously had a problem of sagging breasts (a
complaint among women in the study who had
children). The medical doctor who conducted the
study stated that *all of the women in the study
reported that they were very pleased with the
resulting increase in firmness* and fullness of the
breasts.

5. *More attractive proportioning of the breasts* was
another reported benefit of the method. In the
study cited above the doctor also stated that *all*
participants who previously had breasts of uneven
sizes, reported that their breasts were even in size
by the conclusion of the study.

6. *Spontaneous weight loss* was also reported by
many of the women in this study. Forty-two
percent of the women during the 12 week study
lost weight — and still had significant breast
enlargement.

7. *Smaller waistlines* were delightful by-products of
the program reported by researchers in another
study[4]. In this study careful records were kept of
waist sizes in the tests. The result: all of the
participants reduced their waistlines by the end of
the study, regardless of whether they lost weight or
not. *In addition* to the reduction in waist size, *they*

increased their breast size by an average of <u>approxi-</u>
<u>*mately two inches.*</u>
8. Other positive changes were also reported for a
substantial percentage of the participants. For
example, 78 percent of the participants in one of
the studies reported other positive changes in their
lives[5].

There is another very important benefit of this method
of breast enlargement: *the results are more natural looking
than surgery.* As one medical doctor who uses the method
extensively points out, surgical procedures do not always
produce a totally natural look or feel. He encourages
women to try this method instead of considering the
serious step of surgery[6]. With complication rates as high as
60 percent having been reported for surgery, this recom-
mendation certainly makes sense[7].

It is noteworthy, incidentally, that when breast size is
enlarged by whatever means there are other concomitant
beneficial results. For example, in one follow-up study of
women who had their breasts enlarged, the women
reported increased self-esteem, increased self-confidence,
and feeling happier in all areas of their lives. Many felt that
their interpersonal and marital relationships improved.
They enjoyed their sexual relationships more and reported
increased sexual satisfaction[8].

For those interested in reading the complete details of
the studies on this new breast enlargement method we
refer you to the publications cited in section IV of our
bibliography in the Reading and Study Guide at the back
of the book.

Current Research Findings For a
New Breast Enlargement Method

A CLOSER LOOK
AT THREE OF THE STUDIES

To provide you with greater insight into the potential of this breast enlargement method, let's take a closer look at three of these studies.

Dr. James E. Williams, a clinical psychologist, conducted one of the earlier breast enlargement studies while he was a Counselor at the Gregg-Harrison Mental Health Center in Longview, Texas[9]. The women in this study ranged in age from 18 to 40. Of the group, 53 percent were married and 60 percent of the married women had born children. All of the subjects had reported that their weight had remained approximately constant during the 6 months before the start of the study.

Measurements were taken weekly for the 3 weeks prior to the study to establish a baseline reference for each participant. A careful measuring system was devised using a calibrated measuring apparatus to insure accurate measurements. All measurements were verified by two other participants in the study. The measurements, recorded in fractions of an inch, included both inspired and expired measurements as well as a series of special measurements to verify accurately the changes which were taking place.

Prior to the study the women in the group had measurements ranging from 30.21 inches to 39.08. *After* the study they ranged from 32.33 inches to 41.33. *The average increase for the group was 2.11 inches — with increases ranging as high as 3.54 inches.*

Following the publication of his original study, Dr. Williams continued his research. He later reported another study[10] to determine if the method could be learned from recordings. Dr. Williams reported that he achieved the same positive results with the use of recordings as a convenient teaching aid as he did in his original research. Another unique study was conducted by Richard D. Willard, M.D., of the Cameron Community Hospital and the Institute of Behavioral and Mind Sciences in Indiana[11]. Dr. Willard's study emphasized further *the use of visual imagery,* and the optional convenience of recordings to provide an additional way to learn the method.

The 22 women in Dr. Willard's study ranged in age up to 54 years and all experienced measurable increases in breast size. Five individual breast measurements were used in this study. All were verified by a physician not involved in the design of the experiment. Specific visualizations designed to improve blood circulation included sensing a feeling of warmth in the breasts, as well as the awareness of increased blood flow in the breast area. The participants *practiced the progressive relaxation and imagery at home* once a day. They also kept careful records of their progress.

In this study 63 percent of the women had had children and had complained of pendulous breasts. All reported being very pleased with the increased fullness and firmness they achieved. In addition, all of the women whose breasts were previously uneven in size found that their breasts were even in size by the end of the study. The results also showed that 78 percent of the women in the study reported positive changes in other aspects of their lives.

In a study conducted by Allan R. Staib and D.R. Logan[12] in Houston, the researchers were intrigued by findings in Williams' study that, in addition to breast enlargement, a proportioning effect had occurred. Their study tends to confirm this finding. They reported that the women in their study enjoyed significant reduction in waist sizes, as well as increases in breast size of an average of 2 inches.

Current Research Findings For a
New Breast Enlargement Method

These studies, and the research of others discussed in the next chapter and cited in the bibliography, have contributed greatly to our understanding of this exciting new approach to breast enlargement. They indicate that here at last is a safe, effective, natural way to increase breast size — a method that can help women reach their goals for lovelier, more attractive figures.

CHAPTER THREE
CHAPTER REFERENCES

The detailed publishing information for each of the following chapter references can be found in the bibliography in the Reading and Study Guide at the back of the book. For easy reference the appropriate section of the bibliography is shown in roman numerals following each of the references listed below.

1. Green, A. & E., 1977 (II)
2. Williams, J.E., 1974 (IV)
3. Willard, R.D., 1977 (IV)
4. Staib & Logan, 1977 (IV)
5. Willard, R.D., 1977 (IV)
6. Wilson, D.L., 1979 (IV)
7. Packard, J., 1981 (IV)
8. Baker, J.L., 1974 (IV)
9. Williams, J.E., 1974 (IV)
10. Williams, J.E., 1979 (IV)
11. Willard, R.D., 1977 (IV)
12. Staib & Logan, 1977 (IV)

4

The Significance
Of The New
Discoveries

The initial publication of the clinical studies signaled the advent of a fresh, new approach to breast enlargement. Like most scientific discoveries, the studies represented a link in a chain of events which led to them. Concepts, facts, suggestions, and ideas, from many seemingly disparate directions, funneled together and contributed to our new understanding of this fascinating phenomenon.

In this chapter we examine the significance of the discoveries from three vantage points. First, we look at the current status of the discovery: the initial reactions of scientists and the news media, and the slow dissemination of the information. Then, we glance backwards at the chain of scientists who made significant contributions to the development of the method. After our glance at the past, we look briefly at the future and reflect on the future possibilities that the discovery might bring.

REACTIONS OF SCIENTISTS AND THE
NEWS MEDIA TO THE NEW STUDIES

The significance of these studies, and the results they achieved, were quickly noted in the news media. Here are the reactions of scientists and reporters to those clinical studies:

An M.D. involved in the research states:
"There's no question that the method is here to stay."

An obstetrician-gynecologist reports:
"There is no longer any question about the success and the possibilities regarding this method of breast development."

An M.D. using the method extensively writes:
". . . you will bring about a natural improvement in your figure which is far superior to unnatural surgical procedures, exercise gimmicks, phony nutritional plans, and padded bras."

A popular women's magazine reports:
"Breast Enlargement has been established in two recent studies . . . a non-surgical alternative to breast-augmentation operations."

A leading beauty magazine reports:
". . . Scientists describe how breast growth can be stimulated . . . a safe and sure alternative to surgical build-up of the mammaries — opera-

tions which keep a small army of plastic surgeons busy even at $500 to $2,500 a pair — particularly since reports in the medical literature show that with the bigger bra sizes come new psycho-sexual 'highs'."

A popular fashion magazine reports:
"Today, an increasing number of women are turning to surgery for bigger or shaplier breasts. Now there seems to be a safer, cheaper . . . new alternative on the medical horizon . . . Now there's a promising — and mind-stretching new possibility . . . In a recent 12 week experiment 22 women volunteers ranging in age from 19 to 54 increased their bust measurements by an average of 2 inches (and a maximum of four). . . . All the volunteers noted an unmistakable sense of well-being and confidence in every aspect of their lives . . ."

A best-selling news-weekly reports:
". . . 'we found an average increase in breast size of about 2 inches'. . . Similar experiments around the country achieved equally dramatic results."

An editor of a science journal reports:
"Every female experienced breast size increase — the average increase was two inches . . . and the increase was maintained."

Although the studies did receive coverage in the news media, and limited coverage on network television, the information reached only a fraction of the public. Thus, this remarkable discovery was relegated to the postion of most scientific breakthroughs — known to only a small portion of the public . . . and indeed to only a handful of professionals in the field.

SCIENTIFIC JOURNALS
REPORT ON THE CLINICAL STUDIES

The benefits of this method of breast enlargement, as discussed in the last chapter, are described in depth in the scientific journals. For an in-depth review of those studies we refer you to the articles themselves (see Section IV of the bibliography). Here is a brief indication of the kind of data detailed in those journals.

From the Scientific Journals:

STUDY A *"The mean increase for the group was 2.11 inches. Individual increases ranged from a minimum of 1.0 inches to a maximum of 3.54 inches."*

STUDY B
". . . a desirable alternative to surgical methods of breast augmentation . . . subjects did show an increase in the breast size index between the pretreatment values and the post treatment values. The average increase was 5.00 cm. . . ." (approximately 2 inches).

STUDY C
"In this study, 63 percent of the subjects had had children and complained of pendulous

breasts. These subjects expressed a desire to regain the fullness and contour of the breasts which they had before the pregnancies. All of these subjects reported they were very pleased with the increase in fullness and firmness of their breasts at the end of the study."

One important footnote, especially from a woman's point of view, is that the scientists conducting the studies have now reported, in follow-up work with the women in the studies, that when the method is properly learned the gains are maintained with little or no extra effort. Most women require no maintenance schedule at all; those who do can maintain their gains using the method as infrequently as once every few months. Other researchers, in their own clinical experiences in using the method to help women reach their figure development goals, have verified this fact.[1]

THE SCIENTISTS WHO CONTRIBUTED TO OUR UNDERSTANDING OF THE METHOD

Credit should certainly go to those scientists who contributed so much in this field: to Peter H.C. Mutke, M.D., professor of psychology at the John F. Kennedy University, lecturer at the University of California at Berkeley, and director of the Foundation for Humanistic Medicine and Psychology for his research on breast enlargement through visual imagery techniques and self-image enhancement[2]; to Dr. J.E. Williams, a clinical psychologist for his pioneering study on stimulation of breast growth[3], and for his follow-up study in which he reports achieving the same positive results with the aid of recordings to help teach the method[4]; to R.D. Willard of the Cameron Memorial Community Hospital and the Institute of Behavioral and Mind Sciences in Indiana for his study emphasizing the use of visual imagery and the use of recordings as a teaching tool for the method[5]; to Allen R. Staib and D.R. Logan, under supervision of Dr. James Millham, professor of psychology at the University of Houston, for their examination of the proportioning effect[6], to Dr. George J. Honiotes, an obstetrician-gynecologist at St. Josephs Hospital in Joliet, Illinois, for his corroboration of the statistical averages produced in studies that we cited in chapter 3; to Donald L. Wilson, M.D., founder of The Total Mind Power Institute in San Francisco for his book encouraging women to try this method before considering surgery[7]; to Joan Packard for her research and for her discussion of the method in her book *Natural Breast Enlargement Through Effective Relaxation Techniques*[8]; and to noted clinical psychologist Leslie M. LeCron for reporting on case studies on breast enlargement[9] as early as 1964 as well as for his Journal articles[10] on the subject in 1969.

These scientists, and others, have contributed both directly and indirectly to the current knowledge of the method. The section on Scientific Data in the Reading and Study Guide explores more of the background for these discoveries.

The results in all of these studies have been highly favorable. *And there are no studies, to our knowledge, that have produced any negative evidence or unfavorable outcomes.*

A LOOK AT FUTURE POSSIBILITIES

But the potential benefits of the method may ultimately expand well beyond the specific benefits exhibited in the breast enlargement studies. It's an exciting field for further investigation. As Willard points out, if blood flow can be directed into the breast area with simple visual imagery, perhaps it can be focused in other areas of the body to aid in the treatment of disease, or to help achieve many other physiological improvements. The future implications of the research are certainly exciting to contemplate.

CHAPTER FOUR
CHAPTER REFERENCES

The detailed publishing information for each of the following chapter references can be found in the bibliography in the Reading and Study Guide at the back of the book. For easy reference the appropriate section of the bibliography is shown in roman numerals following each of the references listed below.

1. Wilson, D.L., 1979 (IV)
2. Mutke, P.H.C., 1971 and 1977 (IV)
3. Williams, J.E., 1974 (IV)
4. Williams, J.E., 1979 (IV)
5. Willard, R.D., 1977 (IV)
6. Staib & Logan, 1977 (IV)
7. Wilson, D.L., 1979 (IV)
8. Packard, J., 1981 (IV)
9. LeCron, L.M., 1964 (IV)
10. LeCron, L.M., 1969 (IV)

PART III

Understanding
Bio-Imagery Programming:
What It Is and How It Works

5

Bio-Imagery Programming:
A Practical Program
For Breast Enlargement

While the research studies are fascinating from an academic and scientific point of view, it is the potential of their practical application that is strikingly unique.

Fundamentally, the procedure involves basic learning processes. It is a psychological program, not a medical one. To construct an effective and practical program requires expertise in psychology, and an understanding of the nature of the mind/body relationship.

THE MIND/BODY RELATIONSHIP

The issue of how the mind affects the body is one of the most fascinating problems in modern psychology. Enough volumes have been written on the subject to fill a small library. From endless studies on psychosomatic illness and stress related diseases, to the current trend to explore the fascinating areas of psychosomatic *wellness,* the evidence has been accumulating for more than half a century.

The mind/body relationship has been the focus of countless studies during the last decade. It has been repeatedly demonstrated that individuals can learn to control blood flow, pulse rate, body temperature, and many other body functions[1]. Critical to many of these learning processes is the use of imagery – the visualization of mental pictures in a kind of play-acting scenario which performs on the movie screen of the mind[2]. Its effectiveness is based on the fact that the subconscious mind reacts similarly to both the real (i.e. external) experience and the visual imagery experience (one that is vividly imagined in your mind i.e. internally)[3].

Perhaps the classic example of the mind/body relationship, and certainly the one that has sparked the public's imagination in recent years, is the effect of stress on the individual[4]. The physical effects of a stressful situation, from increased secretions of hormones, to a host of other physiological responses, are well known. What is interesting is that the physiological changes are produced by the particular individual's *perception* of, and reactions to, what precipitates the stress. Even more significantly, people can produce the same physiological responses without actually being in a stressful situation but *just by thinking about it.* For example, if you *think* of some food which is highly distasteful to you, you are likely to have significant reactions in your stomach. A vivid nightmare can trigger physiological changes in the body. An intense scene in a movie can have the same effect – as can thoughts of fear, etc. These are vivid examples of the power of mental pictures. The more vivid and detailed the mental pictures, the more pronounced and prolonged is the physiological response.

BREAST ENLARGEMENT AND BLOOD CIRCULATION

It is this unique ability of mental processes to produce physiological responses which is at the heart of the recent research on breast enlargement.

The complexities of the mind, and the intricacies of the mind/body relationship have been, and probably always will be, an unending topic for further investigation and study. It is easier to measure the results of the processes than to fully understand how they work.

The studies on breast enlargement provide statistics and data. The results have been measured, collated, and analyzed. The prevailing theory of how it works among scientists investigating the phenomena, is that it is the increase in blood circulation in the breast area, produced by the training techniques involved, which stimulates breast growth. Of course, other theories may be postulated to explain the acknowledged facts of breast enlargement achieved through appropriate visual imagery and bodily relaxation, but present evidence supports the theory proposed here. The extensive evidence on the control of bodily processes through learning procedures provides convincing logic to support this explanation.

THE MANY WAYS OF IMPROVING BLOOD CIRCULATION

The control of bodily functions is *not* new — only the

scientific verification of it is new. Bodily functions have been controlled for centuries through meditation and other relaxation techniques. Reports of this kind of bodily control, especially from the eastern cultures, have been heard dating back to our early history. For years scientists scoffed at these tales.

Then, more recently, scientists began to subject the people claiming these abilities to the exacting analysis of the science laboratory. Using the most careful scientific controls, and the best of monitoring equipment, rigorous tests revealed a surprising fact: many of the test subjects had actually taught themselves to alter blood flow, breathing rate, and even their pulse rate.

The fascinating thing was that they had learned these abilities through different means: for some it was meditation; for some yoga; for others visual imagery; and for others it was self-hypnosis or simple self-suggestion.

But these facts were clear:
1. People *can* learn to control their bodily functions.
2. People have learned it through several seemingly different methods.
3. They have, in most cases, learned it without scientific help.

In addition there were certain common denominators among the methods used to learn these simple abilities:
1. All were essentially effortless — that is they used *relaxation techniques* to learn them.
2. All used simple *visual imagery* of some type.

The conclusions are exciting. The methods are simple. They are also non-medical. They are not only relaxing but they are enjoyable. They can be achieved without exotic "trance" states. And they work most effectively when employing visual imagery and relaxation.

Bio-Imagery Programming:
A Practical Program For Breast Enlargement

LEARNING TO ALTER BLOOD FLOW

Concurrently with these discoveries scientists have been analyzing the use of teaching aids to help people learn these simple techniques. These teaching aids employ the use of "feedback" to tell the learner how well he or she is doing. The term biofeedback was coined to describe these learning methods.

In clinics across the country, like the famed Menninger Clinic in Topeka, Kansas, this scene was repeated over and over: people relax comfortably in semi-darkened rooms, listening to tape recordings presenting ideas of total relaxation along with suggested mental pictures designed to help them achieve the appropriate bodily responses. As they relax they listen to tones, or watch dials, which react and change as they succeed in altering their bodily functions.

Since the early beginnings of research into biofeedback, thousands of people have learned to relax and to relieve stress, to change body temperature and relieve migraine headaches, and to reduce high blood pressure through these simple learning methods. A mass of research data has accumulated over the years as Biofeedback Centers have been springing up all over the nation.

But the simple facts about this ability remain:
1. People *can* learn it if they are just shown how[5].
2. Visual imagery and total relaxation are the key elements in learning it.

As Elmer and Alyce Green have reported in their famed studies at the Menninger Clinic[6], even without the use of any biofeedback equipment at all, many people were able to learn the method after practicing it at home by themselves for just a couple of weeks.

BIO-IMAGERY PROGRAMMING: A SCIENTIFICALLY DESIGNED BREAST ENLARGEMENT PROGRAM

In the specific research studies on breast enlargement, discussed in chapters 3 and 4, the results were achieved through the effective use of visual imagery and relaxation techniques. No elaborate biofeedback equipment was needed to achieve the results. Women were taught to use the method by themselves, at home. The studies demonstrated that a properly designed program was really quite simple for women to use — once they are shown how.

But, as we've indicated, properly constructing this kind of learning program requires considerable expertise. A few highly trained psychologists and M.D.'s are now providing private consultations to teach the method. Unfortunately their number is very small. Because of the recency of the research, and because it might not be part of their particular specialty, most professionals may be unaware of this new method. Those professionals interested in learning more about the method will be particularly pleased with the extensive bibliography in the Reading and Study Guide. If you should be fortunate enough to locate one of the handful of professionals specializing in the method, you'll discover another problem however — their skills are highly valuable and their fees, accordingly, very high.

There is another option, however. An internationally known clinical psychologist, whose many contributions to the profession themselves deserve a special biography, has lent his expertise to the design of a comprehensive program based on these specific clinical studies and the related studies detailed in the material that follows. He is widely recognized for his expertise in the fields of clinical psychology, psychotherapy, learning theory and technique, behavioral modification, psychodiagnosis, psycho-physiological behavior, and psychopathology. More of his exceptional background is described in the Reading and Study Guide. The Program, called *New Dimensions,* uses a learning process referred to as *Bio-Imagery Programming.* To our knowledge this Program is the most extensively used Program ever produced. The feedback from users of the *New Dimensions* Program lends additional support to the research studies on the method. Scores of Progress Charts have been examined, analyzed, and collated (see chapters 11 and 12 for samples of these Progress Charts). Correspondence with hundreds of women who have used the Program helps provide additonal input into its effective use. In addition, phone conversations with several hundred of these women has helped to further refine our understanding of the method. The results of this on-going evaluation are tremendously exciting: repeated affirmations of the effectiveness of the procedure, and repeated confirmation of the success of the Program!

By contrast to the expertise required to develop such a program, the actual use of it is amazingly simple! The methods used in the Program are easy-to-understand and easy-to-use. They are based on simple relaxation techniques, and pleasant, enjoyable, visual images. Unlike biofeedback, no elaborate equipment is needed for this method. The Program provides a viable alternative to surgical procedures, and to the great many unproven and ineffective breast enlargement gimmicks marketed for so many years. This logical, sensible approach to breast enlargement produces results that are both natural and natural looking. And it's a technique that women can control themselves — they can use it as long as they wish —

and stop whenever they've reached their goal.

The details of this Program are the subject of the balance of this book. In the next chapter we shall discuss the actual principles involved in *Bio-Imagery Programming*, and we examine more closely how *Bio-Imagery* works.

CHAPTER FIVE
CHAPTER REFERENCES

The detailed publishing information for each of the following chapter references can be found in the bibliography in the Reading and Study Guide at the back of the book. For easy reference the appropriate section of the bibliography is shown in roman numerals following each of the references listed below.

1. Green, A. & E., 1977 (II)
2. Pelletier, K.R., 1977 (II)
3. Hilgard, E.R., 1977 (I)
4. Selye, H., 1974 (II)
5. Green, A. & E., 1977 (II)
6. Green, A. & E., 1977 (II)

6

How *Bio-Imagery Programming* Works

Bio-Imagery Programming is a learning program based on scientifically demonstrated learning principles. In the Program the focus is on improving circulatory processes to assist normal and natural development of the breasts based on the scientific data accumulated in recent clinical studies on breast enlargement. Its methods operate on two levels — learning to influence both physiological processes and, concurrently, the self-image.

The levels are mutually complementary. From what we understand of the process, one seems to act as a catalyst for the other in a kind of reciprocal manner. Each contributes to, and augments the effectiveness of the other. In the *New Dimensions* Program the *"Bio-Images"* — that is, the visual images that are the basis of the learning program — are carefully selected, and balanced, to affect both of these levels.

Based on recent studies on breast enlargement by visual imagery, the images and procedures are carefully woven into the "Scripts" (see chapters 8 & 9) using learning methods that have been proven effective in literally thousands of studies. Each image is carefully painted in the language of the Scripts, with specific physiological responses in mind, using knowledge learned not only from the breast enlargement studies, but from more than a decade of studies on mental control of physiological functions.

Recognizing these two focal areas of the Program, it's helpful to understand what *Bio-Imagery Programming* is and how it works — and especially to understand the ancillary values of improving the self-image.

THE ROLE OF THE SELF-IMAGE

Operationally, *Bio-Imagery Programming* utilizes the untapped potentials already in your mind — including how you think and how you imagine things will be. The process of vividly visualizing again and again and again, through the psychological learning techniques used in the *Bio-Imagery* method, helps to tap these reserves which we already have in our own minds.

The visualizations help you to alter your internalized self-concept, or your self-image. It's this internal self-image that acts as a regulator to control your actions and activities. This regulator functions much like a thermostat to keep your performance within a limited range. Without effective internal regulators most of us really change very little in our lifetimes. And that's one reason why habits seem to be so difficult to break. We continually conform to our own internalized self-image. For example, if we are overweight, we tend to stay overweight. And if we usually over-eat and eat the wrong kinds of foods, we tend to continue to do this. After all, that's how we see ourselves — that's part of our self-image. And everything that we do will be consistent with that image. Unless you change your self-image it is almost impossible to change your eating habits permanently and to attain a permanent loss in weight. But, once you have achieved a realistic and positive self-image, you can quickly learn to do better.

Bio-Imagery works through utilizing effective learning procedures. You see, our minds exercise enormous powers over our lives. We can literally revolutionize our lives by learning to control our thinking. It has been proven time and time again that as individuals we literally become what our self-image suggests. Thoughts tend to become goals. When we recognize that our thoughts do become goals it becomes clear how easy it can be to defeat ourselves. Again, you must first learn how to change your concept of yourself in order to actually change. Visual imagery through visual simulation techniques can promote that new self-concept.

However, positive thinking about your body image is not enough. That is why changing our inner motivation and our self-image can best be achieved by psychologically sound learning techniques such as those used in the *Bio-Imagery Programming* process.

For the vast majority of people it is possible to replace your present self-image with a new, and improved self-image with the utilization of effective learning techinques. Once that happens your desirable goals can be reached. In fact, with an improved self-concept success is virtually assured.

It's clear that improvements in the self-image can be of enormous benefit to any individual. The fact that the specific images used to increase circulation in the breast area provide the added benefit of helping to improve the self-image may be more than coincidental — indeed as we've seen, they may be mutually supportive processes.

The interrelationship of the self-image and the *Bio-Imagery* process is a recurrent theme echoed in the comments of women who have used the Program. These women seem to *think* of themselves differently. And they *feel* differently about themselves. Comments like these reveal the way they view themselves as they progress through the Program:

"This program made me feel better about myself and my appearance. I now have a nicer figure and am proud of myself."

G. B., Kansas City, MO

"I have become more aware of my body as a whole. I no longer think of myself as less of a woman. I seem to have more energy, more vitality. Thank you again for this wonderful experience."

G. H., Reading, PA

"Mental attitude much better — feel better about myself already."

L. M., Richmond, VA

"Please note: Program was continued on a daily basis because it helped me maintain a good feeling about myself. The program was very enjoyable. Thanks."

G. B., Lenexa, KS

The self-image theme seems intricately woven into the

learning process and appears, in many different ways, in the comments of women who have used the Program — a factor that reinforces its important relationship with the process of learning to alter blood flow and increase breast size.

USING *BIO-IMAGERY PROGRAMMING* TO IMPROVE BLOOD CIRCULATION

Through the years science has provided us with many seemingly revolutionary insights into the world around us. Few of these discoveries have surprised scientists as much as the discovery that people could actually *learn* to alter blood flow, pulse rate, body temperature and a host of other body functions.

The key word is learn. That's why *Bio-Imagery* is essentially a learning process. Its particular value, however, is that it uses certain procedures which *accelerate* the learning process, *as well as increase its effectiveness.* This is vitally important since both self-image enhancement, and improving circulation, are concepts that do not respond readily to conventional learning processes. The self-image often seems to be locked in, and any attempts to actively change it seem to run into frequent barriers. This method of improving blood circulation involves a totally new kind of learning orientation. Accordingly, *Bio-Imagery* uses a unique combination of learning procedures carefully programmed to overcome these difficulties and to provide highly effective and pleasurable learning experiences.

THE FOUR SEQUENTIAL PROCEDURES
IN *BIO-IMAGERY PROGRAMMING*

1. Progressive Relaxation

The first of these procedures involves learning deep relaxation. *Progressive Relaxation* is an essential key to rapid and effortless learning, . . . and to the alteration of our inner drives and motivations. More and more scientists are recommending that everyone set aside a quiet period daily for relaxation or meditation time. Typically, they recommend about 15-20 minutes each day for this purpose[1].

The Progressive Relaxation process used in *Bio-Imagery Programming* uses some of the techniques of Autogenic Training[2]. The resulting relaxation from the proper use of the Scripts sets the stage for the learning process. As we have noted, studies on the learning processes involved in altering blood flow, body temperature, etc. indicate that the best results are accomplished in a relaxed state of focused awareness[3].

2. Visualization

A second factor that is extremely important in *Bio-Imagery* is Visualization — using words, pictures, and emotions to provide vivid, visual mental pictures of your goal[4]. These mental pictures repeated over and over again, in a relaxed frame of mind, help you create a new self-image — to see yourself in a different way. They are like a rehearsal for our daily lives — a practice session[5]. And since scientists have proven that *the subconscious mind cannot distinguish between a real experience and one that is vividly imagined in great detail*[6], these mental pictures become a part of our lives and can affect our habits and our internalized self-image.

3. Reinforcement

The third important factor is Reinforcement[7]. After all we've spent most of our life developing our present self-image. Using the *Bio-Imagery* method *consistently* and following the reinforcement program suggested will enable you to change your self-image. Each time you follow the Program you will be making more and more progress as the Program becomes easier and easier, and the experiences and images become more and more a part of you. Remember you're after a *lifetime* of self-confidence and assurance. Inner motivations are the key — motivations that are internalized through words, pictures, and emotions used repeatedly, while you are in a relaxed frame of mind.

4. Perceptive Feedback

The fourth important factor is Perceptive Feedback. Feedback is another essential key to learning[8]. Feedback is simply a process of guided learning that emphasizes correct responses. *Bio-Imagery* helps you to learn how to make these proper responses.

* * * * *

Put all of these factors together and you have the essence of how *Bio-Imagery Programming* works. By following the simple learning program for a few minutes a day, you can learn to influence your bodily processes, change your inner motivations — and to change your self-image. The road map for that learning program is the subject of Part IV of this book: *"How to Use the Program: A Step-By-Step Guide."* The easy-to-follow instructions in Part IV transform the intricate maze of knowledge on which the Program is based into a simple and easy-to-use Program to help you reach your goal for a lovelier, more attractive figure.

CHAPTER SIX
CHAPTER REFERENCES

The detailed publishing information for each of the following chapter references can be found in the bibliography in the Reading and Study Guide at the back of the book. For easy reference the appropriate section of the bibliography is shown in roman numerals following each of the references listed below.

1. Benson, H., 1975 (II)
2. Schultz, J.H., 1959 (II)
3. Green, A. & E., 1977 (II)
4. Pelletier, K.R., 1977 (II)
5. Bry, A., 1978 (II)
6. Hilgard, E.R., 1977 (I)
7. Skinner, B.F., 1971 (II)
8. Leitenberg, H., 1969 (II)

PART IV

How To Use The Program: A Step-By-Step Guide

7

Your Introduction to The *Bio-Imagery* Scripts

Now that we have discussed the scientific basis for this revolutionary new breast enlargement method, it's time to learn the simple instructions for using it.*

* The reader should understand that this publication is designed to provide accurate and authoritative information in regards to this specific program. It is sold with the understanding that the publisher is not engaged in rendering medical advice or other professional service. If medical advice is required, the services of a competent physician should be sought.

It is always advisable to discuss any self-improvement program with your doctor. Scientific evidence indicates that the techniques used in this Program clearly will work with normal, healthy women. If you have any questions about any physical abnormality regarding your breasts, or your health in general, consult your physician. Although this Program is considered safe for all women in good health, there may be an unknown medical reason why your doctor would feel that it is inappropriate for you. Since you are starting a new beautifying program, start with a physical check-up. The radiant glow of good health is always an important factor in your total attractiveness.

In the preceding chapters we presented the following points:

1. The method is based on sound scientific data and it's a method that really works.
2. It works by teaching simple learning procedures which help to increase blood circulation in the breast area and thus stimulate natural, normal breast growth.
3. The methods are mastered through the use of "Scripts" which employ a four-phase learning program:
   A. Progressive Relaxation — to speed the learning process.
   B. Visualization — to facilitate increased blood circulation in the breast area.
   C. Reinforcement — to insure and maintain rapid learning, and to retain what has been learned.
   D. Perceptive Feedback — to help in monitoring and improving the learning process.
4. The method is amazingly simple to learn.

This last point is the best part of all. Frequently, scientific data and scientific explanation sound complicated. But it's hard to make the actual use of this Program complicated! *Because all one has to do is to read a Script, or rehearse it in one's mind, or listen to a recording of it, or have someone else read it to you and then follow the simple, relaxing suggestions that one thinks about, reads, or hears.* You simply do this daily according to the schedule shown on the Progress Chart. (You can even learn to use the method without the Scripts or recordings.) That's it! There are no exercises. No devices. No diets or drugs. Just a simple, natural program that works!

How do you use the Scripts? This chapter will help you decide the best way for you.

Your Introduction To The Bio-Imagery Scripts

What do the Scripts say? Read Scripts One and Two in chapters 8 and 9 to get an idea.

How often do you use them? Chapter 10, *How to use the Program and the Progress Chart,* answers that question. Chapters 11 and 12 contain actual Progress Charts of women who have used the Program.

For additional concrete suggestions about getting the most out of the Program, see chapter 13, *Maximizing Your Results* and chapter 14, *The Maximum Effects Program.*

And if you have any other questions about the Program, chapter 15, *Questions and Answers About the Method,* should answer them.

Remember the important thing — it's *simple* to use. Just read, or listen, to the Scripts according to the schedule and follow the suggestions in the Scripts. That's all there is to it. So don't make it complicated. Just read this section of the book right now so that you can start your Program as quickly as possible!

WAYS OF USING THE SCRIPTS

The key to the *Bio-Imagery Programming* process is the *Bio-Imagery* Script. For it is the Script that is the heart of the learning program. The Script utilizes proven learning techniques and the four sequential elements of the method: progressive relaxation, visualization, reinforcement, and perceptive feedback. The Script teaches the appropriate visualizations that have been shown in clinical studies to increase breast size by improving circulatory processes, while simultaneously enhancing the self-image.

Since the Script is essentially a learning program, your goal should be to learn the process in an easy and relaxed manner.

There are four ways the Scripts can be learned:

1. The first, and most obvious method, is to read the appropriate Script to yourself according to the schedule described in the section on the Progress Chart (chapter 10). Just sit back in a soft easy chair and read the Script *slowly and silently to yourself.* As you do, follow the suggestions and instructions given in the Script — except, of course, you will be keeping your eyes open for the full reading. Be sure that you are seated comfortably, and that you are away from all distractions. Each time you read the Script (following the schedule on the Progress Chart) you will be reinforcing the learning process.

2. The second method is to study the Script thoroughly until you have learned its basic concepts, and then review the complete Scripts in your own mind as completely and vividly as possible — again according to the schedule shown on the Progress Chart. Since the process is simply a learning process, this method can be surprisingly effective* once you have a thorough understanding of the information in the Script and then use it consistently.

3. The third method is to have a friend read the Scripts to you in a slow, relaxed, easy-going tone of voice. Some women find the Program is most

---

*The following interesting letter provides an example of using the method in this way. It was received from a woman whose only knowledge of the Script was that she heard a recording of it *just one time* (her record player broke after the first time she played the record): "...I was able to do the programming on my own once I grasped the idea ... each breast has enlarged at least 2½ inches and I am absolutely delighted. Thank you!"

L.D., Arlington, TX

effective if the Script is read to them by a man. Others feel more comfortable listening to a woman's voice. And some enjoy an occasional change from a male to a female voice to lend variety to the Program. Although, in other kinds of learning programs some scientists feel that both men and women are more responsive to the voices of the opposite sex, for this Program you should determine for yourself which you prefer.

4. The fourth, and perhaps most convenient way, is to listen to a recorded version of the Script. More and more people these days are enjoying the effortless convenience of Talking Books — written information and material that has been recorded on tape or LP records. They have become especially popular for material that is to be learned, since recordings can be listened to again and again so easily and effortlessly. Some women prefer the use of the Talking Book concept when learning the *Bio-Imagery* Scripts. If you prefer this method, we suggest that you read the Script first, at least once, and then use the Talking Book recordings for subsequent sessions. People learn by different routes, but the Talking Book concept is highly effective for most because it is a passive, relaxing procedure, and because it is very vivid. And it can help many people learn *faster* and assimilate the learning process more *completely*. (In using the recorded versions of the Scripts, as in using the other three methods, it's best to be away from any distractions. For privacy you may prefer to listen to the recordings with an inexpensive earphone or set of headphones. These are available from most stores that carry record players or tape recorders.)

It should be noted that the process of recording the Script on tape or records in no way confers any magical qualities to the recording. The essential core of the learning program is in the *written* Scripts. As you have seen, this book is designed so it can be used totally independently of any recordings. A recording is simply a convenient and useful learning tool. It can simplify and accelerate the learning of the information, just as it can expedite the assimilation of other information recorded in the same way*. (If you prefer to learn the method from a recording and you do not already have one, recorded versions of the Scripts are available from New Directions, Inc. These recordings are available in professionally recorded form on either 12" LP records or cassettes. No medical claims of any sort are made for the recordings. For information on these spoken transcriptions of the written Scripts write to New Directions, Inc., Suite 208, Dept. BK-200, 161 Ottawa N.W., Grand Rapids, Michigan 49503.)

Although many people may prefer the ease of sitting back and listening to a recording, both Scripts are written so that they can be used easily by *any* of the four possible methods that we have presented.

To emphasize: you can use any one of the four learning methods described here, or, any *combination* of the four methods. In fact, you may find it beneficial to vary the method that you use occasionally.

*Extensive studies on learning theory and methods have demonstrated the value of recordings in the learning of information, and this has contributed to the growing popularity of learning information in this convenient way. It's interesting to note that two clinical studies on this breast enlargement method have demonstrated that recordings could be helpful as a learning aid in helping to learn the process: the study by R.D. Willard[1]; and a study by J.E. Williams[2] that he conducted several years after his original study[3]. Other professionals using the method have also found the use of recordings helpful (Wilson[4] and Packard[5]).

THE *BIO-IMAGERY* SCRIPTS:
AN OVERVIEW

Script One is called *The Basic Program.* It contains all of the ingredients for using the Program successfully: progressive relaxation, visualization (including *Bio-Images* 1, 2, and 3) reinforcement, and perceptive feedback. As such it could, if desired, be used exclusively throughout the Program. However, the effective utilization of two additional Scripts can help you to accelerate your progress, help you to enhance the effectiveness of the Program, and help you maximize your results. They add interest and variety as you progress toward your goal.

Script Two is *The Accelerated Program.* At first glance Script Two may seem quite similar to Script One. However, as you actually begin to use Script Two you'll find that the relaxation process is more advanced, and the imagery more vivid and intense. The step-up in detail enhances the effectiveness of the learning program. Most important of all, however, is that Script Two uses 3 totally different *Bio-Images* (*Bio-Images* 4, 5, and 6). These new *Bio-Images* provide additional mental pictures to help expedite the learning process. To accelerate and enhance learning the method, begin alternating Scripts One and Two every other day any time after week 4. If you feel that you are making substantial progress in learning to relax and in the use of the imagery, you can, if you wish, introduce Script Two even earlier in your Program.

A third Script, called *The Maximum Effects Program,* is discussed in Part V of the book. It can be used once or twice a week as an alternate to the other Scripts, or as an "extra" anytime throughout the entire Program. It is especially helpful for insuring rapid progress, overcoming "plateaus", etc. For more information on the use of this Script see chapters 13 and 14.

The next two chapters contain the complete text for Script One and Script Two. As you read these Scripts for the first time you will see how the findings from the research studies are utilized in the *Bio-Imagery Programming* process. More importantly, you will gain an understanding of how the use of visual imagery helps people learn how to improve blood circulation in various parts of the body.

Keep in mind, as you read these Scripts, that while it may *seem* incredible that visualizations, such as those used in the Scripts, can actually help you improve blood circulation in specific parts of the body, that this finding is now well-corroborated by extensive scientific data. And while it also may seem incredible that these methods can help increase breast size, the cited studies have demonstrated that breast enlargement is almost always achieved by these methods.

After you have read the Scripts in chapters 8 and 9, you'll want to learn just how to use them and how to get started on your own personal Program. Specific instructions are contained in chapter 10.

As you proceed, you will also find it helpful to review the progress of other women who have used the Program (see chapters 11 and 12). Comments discussing each chart are included to help you benefit from the experiences of others.

But for now, your next step in getting started is to read the Scripts and the instructions. The next three chapters introduce you to those Scripts and show you precisely how to use them.

CHAPTER SEVEN
CHAPTER REFERENCES

The detailed publishing information for each of the following chapter references can be found in the bibliography in the Reading and Study Guide at the back of the book. For easy reference the appropriate section of the bibliography is shown in roman numerals following each of the references listed below.

1. Willard, R.D., 1977 (IV)
2. Williams, J.E., 1979 (IV)
3. Williams, J.E., 1974 (IV)
4. Wilson, D.L., 1979 (IV)
5. Packard, J., 1981 (IV)

8

The Basic
Program

NEW DIMENSIONS® II
BIO-IMAGERY PROGRAMMING™
Figure Enhancement System

THE BASIC PROGRAM*
Script One

This Program to assist you in developing yourself is a simple and effective method. You will find it easy and enjoyable. Just let yourself relax and follow the simple procedures.

The Basic Program

First, make yourself as comfortable as you can by sitting back in a soft easy chair, or by lying comfortably on your back in your bed or on a couch. Take a moment to loosen any tight clothing. Take off your shoes so that you will be totally comfortable. Place your arms in a comfortable and relaxed position and begin to relax the muscles of your whole body. Now, as you begin to relax, think carefully about the instructions you are reading or hearing.* If you are listening to these instructions, or using them from memory, close your eyes so that you'll be even more relaxed.

While you are relaxed, simply follow the instructions and suggestions that you read or hear (or think about from memory). You will find it easy to follow these *suggestions* and *instructions.*

As you learn to relax and enjoy these suggestions you will find that you become even more comfortable and have an enjoyable experience. The Program is easy and will be natural. It will require no special effort. Just relax and let it happen and the Program will work automatically. Remember, you can be confident that the Program works. You will find it is easy if you just *let it happen almost by itself.* The key words are: let yourself feel comfortable; let yourself relax and enjoy it; you will find it *pleasant and easy.*

*RECORDED VERSIONS OF SCRIPTS ONE AND TWO:
The current popularity of Talking Books demonstrates that many people prefer the convenience of learning information from recordings. Although a tape or record is not essential for learning the method, it can expedite the process of learning this information just as it can any other information presented this way. No medical claims of any sort are made for these recordings. For those who prefer this convenience, these Scripts are available in professionally recorded form in a choice of either 12" LP record or cassette. For information write to: New Directions, Inc., Suite 208, Dept. BK-200, 161 Ottawa, N.W., Grand Rapids, Michigan 49503.

The next few minutes is a time to relax totally. It is a time to let the stresses of the day fade away and let the daily tensions drain away. *Your Program* will help you to feel more refreshed and feel more effective — even more alive and vibrant. *As you relax,* you will learn automatically to feel more and more comfortable. You will find that each time you listen to or read this Program and relax, it becomes easier and easier.

You are already learning to relax and feel more comfortable. You have already learned the first lesson without effort as you learn to relax. In time you will learn to relax quickly and effectively with or without the Script.

Now, as you lie or sit comfortably, you are beginning to learn to relax quickly, easily, and effectively. You will begin to find that you breathe more easily and effortlessly. You can learn to relax easily as you say to yourself the words, *"I can relax now and breathe comfortably. This is my time to relax."* Just *thinking* these words helps you to relax. You are learning to use these words as your own, personal Program. You can even reduce these words to simply "relax now" to let you drain the tensions of your body away, and enjoy deeper and deeper relaxation. Listening to the recording, or reading this Script, or just mentally thinking the ideas presented here, helps this process of relaxing and enjoying. So say to yourself, as you do: "Just RELAX NOW: RELAX NOW: RELAX NOW." See how it becomes easier and easier and more and more pleasant.

Now you are learning to relax and feel comfortable. Good. Let the strains and tensions in your body *drain* away, slip away. You feel more comfortable.

Now as you are learning to relax and have pleasant feelings and thoughts, you can enjoy relaxation even more. Just take two long, comfortable breaths and exhale slowly, and comfortably. (PAUSE) Now do this again and *feel the tension just draining away.* (PAUSE) Now, you can *visualize or see in your mind's eye,* a peaceful, relaxing picture of yourself as you feel yourself *drifting* into a deeper state of relaxation. Now take one more breath, slowly and comfortably. *Feel* yourself drifting, carefree; *see* yourself drifting, floating, more and more relaxed. Enjoy this feeling. Just drift — comfortable, relaxed, and *carefree.*

*   *   *   *   *

Begin now to relax *ALL* the muscles of your body — to let them become loose and as limp as possible. Let's work with one leg — choose either leg and as you follow your Program first tighten the muscles of that leg — making the leg *feel* tight and rigid all over. Keep your leg muscles tight for a moment. (PAUSE) Now, let your leg muscles begin to relax from your toes up to your hip. Focus your attention, first, on your toes, letting them relax ... then on the muscles of your lower leg, letting them relax ... then the muscles in your thigh, letting them relax. That's good. Now, tighten up all the muscles of your leg again, and hold them tight for awhile ... then, let them relax, as before, starting with your toes, and going up until your leg is quite relaxed. OK, that's fine.

Now, tighten up your stomach muscles; hold them that way for a moment. (PAUSE) Now, let your stomach muscles relax. It will be easy to relax your stomach muscles if, first, you tighten your stomach muscles, and then relax them — letting them go. See how good this feels!

Now do the same thing with your chest and breathing

muscles. Again, it will be easy to relax your chest and breathing muscles if, first, you tighten them and then relax them — letting them go. Tighten them first; now let them relax. (PAUSE) Feel the relaxation.

Now focus on your shoulders and your shoulder muscles. Tighten them by pulling your shoulders back; *feel* how tight they are. Now, let the muscles of your shoulders relax. *Feel* the relaxation in your back.

Now stretch your neck and tighten those muscles. Again, relax. (PAUSE)

Now do the same thing with the muscles in your arms from the shoulders right down to your fingertips. First tighten these muscles, making your arms and fingers tight and rigid; now, let your muscles from your shoulders right down to your fingertips relax.

Now, tighten up your whole face. Hold your face that way for a moment. Tight. Tighter. Now relax all the muscles of your face and feel the comfort in your face. Now you can feel even more relaxed all over.

*   *   *   *   *

Your whole body is relaxing. Relaxation is so pleasant and so comfortable. Let go completely and enjoy it. As you relax your whole body, all tension seems to drain away and you soon find a new sense of comfort and well-being. Even your breathing is more relaxed. You begin to feel relaxed all over, and a bit drowsy, and more and more comfortable. Your whole body is relaxed, and your mind is at ease and you feel comfortable. (PAUSE)

Now you can attain *even greater* relaxation of your body and your mind. You can use your mind to help you. It's so easy. Just imagine that you are standing at the top of a very pleasant stairway with nice colors and soft carpeting. This will become your 10-step stairway to even more comfort and relaxation. Now, *in your imagination* see yourself walking down this stairway, slowly, step-by-step, and as you walk take each step in time with the count. And as we count, see yourself stepping down with each count, step-by-step, walking down to greater comfort and more relaxation.

Step #1, relax. You begin to feel so relaxed and drowsy.

Now step down, #2, and feel more drowsy and relaxed, more comfortable.

Now #3. Getting more drowsy and relaxed.

#4. Getting more and more comfortable and relaxed.

#5. You can feel the *soft carpeting* and feel more relaxed, more comfortable.

#6. Relaxed. Comfortable.

#7. More drowsy, more relaxed, more comfortable.

#8. Getting more relaxed, more comfortable.

#9. Relaxed. Comfortable.

#10. So drowsy, so comfortable, so relaxed. Your body and your mind are both relaxed.

Now continue to relax, more and more. You feel comfortable and relaxed. As you think clearly and effortlessly of every word, your mind and your body feel more and more relaxed. You are breathing in a more relaxed and comfortable manner. With each breath you take you feel more relaxed, alert, and more comfortable.

You are learning to relax very comfortably. Just continue to relax, rest, and to read or listen.

Now we will begin to use mental pictures to help your body become more sensitive and responsive. These pictures will teach your body how to function more effectively.

BIO-IMAGE #1

Picture in your mind how your body looked when you were about 12 years of age. Picture what your whole body looked like — your breasts, your arms, and your legs. Try to see yourself as your body looked. Focus on this mental picture of your body. In your mind's eye you are now 12 years old. You can see your figure. You can see your breasts. Remember some of the disappointment you felt when you saw your body? *Bio-Imagery* can help change that.

As you look at your picture when you were about 12 years of age and *feel* how you looked, begin to see your body changing. In your mind begin to see your figure developing; developing slowly, but developing beautiful proportions. *See* your breasts getting larger and firmer. *Imagine* it happening. *Feel* the blood coursing into your breasts as they begin to grow and develop. As you breathe deeply, *feel* the energy going into your breasts. You can begin to feel your breasts actually growing larger, fuller, firmer. Now you can *feel* your breasts pushing outward. As you *see* your breasts growing larger and firmer, you *feel* a *pleasant tightness* of the skin over the breasts. They are growing, growing, growing.

See how your figure is becoming more attractive. As you see and feel your breasts developing, you can *feel* how your waistline begins to feel more trim. As your breasts develop, your body proportions change, and you begin to feel proud of your figure.

Your body is beginning to grow and develop as you would like. It will continue to develop as more blood courses into your breasts, as your breasts become larger and firmer and as your figure becomes more lovely.

NOW you can picture yourself as you will be by the

end of this Program. In your mind, visualize yourself as you step out of the shower and stand in front of a full length mirror. See how much larger your breasts have become — see how lovely you look with larger, more attractive breasts and a smaller, lovelier waistline. See yourself *vividly, clearly* — with your beautifully improved, beautifully proportioned figure.

Now you have completed your practice with this picture which we shall call *Bio-Image* #1. It has already initiated the process of physiological change. You have begun to see and to feel how you can look.

Now you can relax even more and your body and your mind can feel comfortable, and pleasantly, deeply relaxed.

BIO-IMAGE #2

And now we can turn to *Bio-Image* #2.

You are learning to relax ever more fully and your mind is focusing on your breasts. And now you can focus all of your attention on your breasts. Just imagine now that a warm, moist, comfortable towel is being placed on your breasts. *Feel the warmth* penetrating into your skin and into your breasts. *Feel* how comfortable and how relaxing the warmth is. As you *feel* the warmth in your breasts you can begin to *feel more blood flowing into your breasts,* stimulating their growth and vibrancy. As the blood flows into your breasts they feel healthier, more vibrant, firmer. You can feel the growth process beginning. Now, focus your attention on the blood pulsating from your heart into your breasts. It is a pleasant, comfortable, warm feeling. A pleasant pulsation of blood enlarging your breasts. A warm, growing sensation. Your breasts are beginning to grow from the inside, to feel fuller, firmer, more attractive.

See how comfortable your breasts feel and how good you feel about your body development and how much more comfortable it makes you feel.

Your mind will continue to help your blood flow to your breasts so that they can continue to grow fuller and larger and firmer.

BIO-IMAGE #3

And NOW a third *Bio-Imagery* picture will assist you even more in developing larger, fuller, and firmer breasts.

Imagine yourself with the figure you've always dreamed of — and being tremendously proud of every part of your figure and especially of your breasts. You can feel confident and proud of the lovely breasts that you are developing. People will admire your figure, the figure of a proud and confident woman. There is no guilt connected with a beautiful figure, only confidence and mature pride. A lovely woman is a proud woman. A woman with lovely breasts is a confident woman. You will like yourself, even admire yourself, more and more as you see your breasts developing and as people respond to your beautiful figure. It is a good feeling, a relaxed feeling, a feeling of great confidence.

As you think of *Bio-Image #3* you are in a very deep state of total relaxation. Very comfortable. Very relaxed. And your mind focuses on, and remembers, the 3 *Bio-Images*. Twice daily you will enjoy relaxing for a short period of time and vividly picture the 3 *Bio-Images*.

Bio-Image #1 — Your breasts growing and enlarging, becoming fuller and firmer, lovelier, just as they would when a girl grows from 12 years of age and then pictures her perfectly lovely figure, as yours will be, at the conclusion of your Bio-Imagery Programming with larger, firmer breasts.

Bio-Image #2 — A sense of warmth, pulsation, and increased blood flow which is helping your breasts to grow larger, lovelier.

and

Bio-Image #3 — A feeling of great pride and confidence about your lovely figure.

Twice each day, you will enjoy relaxing and setting aside a brief period of time to visualize these 3 *Bio-Images.* And you will enjoy reading or listening to this Script on a regular basis.

Each time that you read or listen to this Script you will enter a deeper, more comfortable stage of relaxation. Each time you read or listen you will find that you relax more quickly. And each time that you say to yourself the words "RELAX NOW" you will be able to relax completely, immediately, and will then visualize the 3 *Bio-Images.* This script, and the 3 *Bio-Images,* used consistently, will help assure you of achieving your figure goals. Your breasts will grow larger, firmer, fuller, more attractive, and your waistline will become slimmer. Following this Program on a regular basis will help you to relax, relieve stress and tension, and enable you to achieve your figure goals. Practice the *Bio-Imagery* technique with the 3 *Bio-Images* twice daily, and you will enjoy the benefits of a lovelier, more attractive figure.

REMEMBER THE ELEMENTS:
1. Read the Script or listen to the recording on a regular schedule.
2. Twice daily say the words "RELAX NOW" and vividly picture the 3 *Bio-Images*.
3. Each time that you do, it will become easier, faster, and more automatic.

These elements are your key to a lovelier figure.

And now, to conclude this Script count to five after which you will feel wide awake, happy, and refreshed.
1. Feeling good, feeling pleasant, getting up.
2. More alert, refreshed, enthusiastic.
3. Stretching your arms and legs and body — feeling good, refreshed.
4. Eyes wide open, feeling wonderful.
5. More alert. Feeling good. Feeling refreshed. Feeling vigorous.

9
The Accelerated Program

NEW DIMENSIONS ® *II*
BIO-IMAGERY PROGRAMMING ™
Figure Enhancement System

THE ACCELERATED PROGRAM
Script Two

Now that you've learned the basic features of the Program, and certain physiological processes have begun to have their effect, it's time to strengthen these processes to achieve maximal results. By simply following the procedures, you will find that it's easy to achieve your personal goals and have a beautiful figure.

Sit back in your soft, easy chair, or lie comfortably on your back on your bed or couch, and let yourself relax. Take off your shoes and loosen any tight clothing so as to be more comfortable. Place your arms in a comfortable and relaxed position and let your whole body relax. Say to yourself: "Relax *now*. Relax *now.*" Now, as you continue to relax, read (or listen to)* the following instructions. If you are listening to these instructions, or following them from memory, close your eyes so that you'll be even more relaxed.

Remember, this is a time to let the stresses and tensions fade away — to make your body vibrant and alive — comfortable and relaxed.

Since you have already learned a great deal about the art of relaxing, it will be easier and easier to relax more quickly and more deeply. You will find that you breathe easily and effortlessly. Keep thinking to yourself: "Relax now. This is my time to relax." Just thinking these words helps you to relax more deeply. So relax and let the tensions continue to drain away.

Now we will repeat some of the things we learned before, making them more and more effective. First, take a long, deep breath, hold it for a moment — now, exhale slowly, comfortably. (PAUSE) *Feel* the relaxation and *feel* the tension drain away. Now do this over again, and while taking a deep breath, visualize in your mind a peaceful relaxing picture of yourself as you seem to drift in space. As you exhale, feel yourself *drifting, drifting, drifting.* Now take still another deep breath, hold it for a moment,

---

*RECORDED VERSIONS OF SCRIPTS ONE AND TWO:
The current popularity of Talking Books demonstrates that many people prefer the convenience of learning information from recordings. Although a tape or record is not essential for learning the method, it can expedite the process of learning this information just as it can any other information presented this way. No medical claims of any sort are made for these recordings. For those who prefer this convenience, these Scripts are available in professionally recorded form on a choice of either 12" LP record or cassette. For information write to: New Directions, Inc., Suite 208, Dept. BK-200, 161 Ottawa N.W., Grand Rapids, Michigan 49503.

exhale, and again *see* and *feel* yourself drifting — becoming *more relaxed,* more *comfortable.* Enjoy the feeling. Just drift and relax, *carefree.*

* * * * *

As you relax comfortably, you can learn to relax all the muscles of your body even more than before. Let's work with one leg — choose either leg. First tighten all the muscles of this leg. Raise your leg slightly, meanwhile *tightening* all the muscles of your leg — in *your thigh,* in *your calf,* and in *your toes.* Tighten them more and more until your leg is *rigid — tighter, tighter, tighter.* Keep your whole leg tight and rigid *for a moment longer.* Now, lower the leg and let it relax, from your toes all the way up to your hip. As you relax the muscles of your leg, *feel* the tension drain out, *feel* the comfortable feeling in your leg. That's good. *Feel* the tension drain out. *Enjoy this feeling* as you rest comfortably for a moment. Now, let's do this again: tightening *all the muscles* of the same leg, raising the leg slightly, making the leg so rigid, *tight, tighter.* Hold it for a moment. (PAUSE) Now, as you lower the leg, relax all the muscles, feel the relaxation, feel the tension drain away, feel your whole body becoming more comfortable and relaxed. Enjoy this feeling as you relax. OK that's fine.

Now we will learn to relax the muscles of our stomach so as to relax our whole body even more. First, *tighten up* the muscles of your stomach by pulling your stomach in more and more. Hold it this way for a moment. Your stomach muscles are now quite tight. Now *relax* your stomach muscles. Let your stomach expand to its normal position. As your stomach muscles relax, you relax. You feel more comfortable and more relaxed.

Now let's relax our shoulder muscles. First tighten the muscles of your shoulders by pulling your shoulders back, *tighter, tighter.* Hold them that way for a moment. (PAUSE) Feel how tight they are. Now, let the shoulder muscles relax. *Feel* the relaxation in your shoulders. *Feel* the relaxation spreading to your back. Relax and enjoy this.

Now, as you are getting more and more relaxed, let us learn to relax our neck muscles. First, tighten your neck muscles by stretching your neck and pulling your head back, until your neck muscles feel quite tight and rigid. Hold them this way for a moment. (PAUSE) Now let your neck muscles relax and *feel* how relaxed and comfortable your neck is.

Now, let's relax the muscles in one arm — choose either arm. First *tighten* all the muscles of your arm by *stretching* your arm and raising it slightly, tightening the muscles in your upper arm, in your forearm, and in your fingers, stretching them out — *tighter, tighter, tighter.* Keep your arm and fingers tight and rigid for a moment. *Feel* the tightness. (PAUSE) Now relax your arm and finger muscles as you lower your arm. *Feel* the comfort and relaxation. Relax and enjoy this feeling.

Now, let's relax our facial muscles, First, *tighten* your facial muscles, tightening your mouth, feeling the tightness in your mouth, in your cheeks and in your neck. Hold your face like this for a moment. Now, just let your facial muscles relax, and feel the warmth and relaxation in your whole face.

Now that you have relaxed many of the muscles of your body, as you relax, see how easily you breathe; how comfortable your whole body feels; how comfortable you feel. Enjoy this wonderful, comfortable feeling. (PAUSE)

*   *   *   *   *

Now you can relax both your mind and your body. It's so easy. Your mind can help your body and your body can help your mind. Imagine now that you are standing at the top of a very pleasant-looking stairway, a stairway with nice colors and with soft, soft carpeting. See this stairway in *your mind's eye.* This 10-step stairway will now become your stairway to greater comfort of mind and body. Now, in your *vivid imagination,* we shall walk down this stairway to greater comfort and relaxation, step-by-step, slowly and comfortably. Let us step down as we count. Step down #1 into the soft carpet and relax.

Now, step down #2, and relax even more, getting more comfortable, more relaxed.

Step #3, into the soft carpeting and feeling more and more comfortable.

Step #4, comfortable.

Step #5, getting more and more relaxed.

Step #6, more comfortable, more relaxed.

Step #7, so comfortable, so relaxed.

Step #8, more and more relaxed, more comfortable.

Step #9, relaxed, comfortable.

Step #10, the last step, comfortable, the step to deepest comfort and deepest relaxation.

See how both your body and your mind have become so relaxed. With each breath you take you feel more relaxed, alert, and more comfortable.

Now, as you are relaxing, your body and your mind feel completely relaxed. You feel content, sure of yourself, at ease with the world. Just relax and enjoy it. As you read or listen your body will learn to respond effortlessly and function more efficiently. And as you continue to relax we will see some pictures in our mind. These pictures will instruct your body how to behave and function — easily, relaxedly, and without effort.

These pictures will be called *Bio-Images* 4, 5, and 6. Like the other *Bio-Images* you have been learning, these mental pictures will help your body become more sensitive and responsive and to function more effectively.

BIO-IMAGE #4

Picture in your mind this scene: You are lying comfortably on a pleasant, sunny beach. You are by yourself in a beautiful, private, secluded spot. Your eyes are closed and you are relaxing comfortably as you feel the pleasant *warmth* from the sun. You feel warm, comfortable, and pleasant.

As you relax you notice how *warm* and *pleasant* your breasts feel. You *feel* the friendly warmth of the sun spreading the sensation of warmth all over your breasts. Your breasts begin to tingle and you *feel* them getting larger, fuller, firmer. Your breasts are growing. You can feel them swelling upward toward the sun. You *feel* them getting larger. Your breasts are growing and becoming more and more beautiful each day. You enjoy this pleasant feeling of growth. You can sense them growing — you feel them getting larger and you enjoy this pleasant, tingling feeling of warmth and growth as your breasts swell and grow to beautiful, attractive, proportions.

Now, as you relax, enjoying the warmth, your mind drifts back to the time when your breasts were just beginning to grow. You see in your mind how you looked when you were younger. You remember how you looked and felt when you were younger. You remember hoping that your body would develop into beautiful, attractive proportions. Now, as you watch, you see your breasts starting to grow. But *this time* your breasts are growing *much larger* than they did back then. And as you watch you see the image of yourself beginning to change. You *see* your breasts growing larger, lovelier. You *feel* it happening. You *feel the blood flowing* into your breasts making your breasts larger. Your breasts are growing and developing beautiful proportions. You feel pleased and satisfied with the attractive new growth of your breasts.

And now you see a *new picture* of yourself as you will look at the end of this Program. You see how large and full and lovely your breasts have become. You *see* and *feel* how attractive you are. Your breasts are larger and more beautiful. You feel more attractive, more poised, more self-confident. You enjoy the great sense of pride that you feel as you see this lovely new image of yourself. Now as you visualize these mental pictures you continue to enjoy the warmth from the sun. The warmth of the sun feels *so good*. The sun has helped your breasts to grow, and your figure to reach beautiful new proportions.

BIO-IMAGE #5

Now, as you relax, your mind flows to thoughts of the gentle *rhythm* of your body. You enjoy the smooth, relaxing *rhythm* of your breathing. With each breath you take your breasts begin to swell. You *feel* your breasts swelling, growing. Your breasts feel larger, fuller, firmer. With each breath you take you feel your breasts getting *larger, lovelier*. The oxygen you breath is traveling your bloodstream into the breast area. You *feel* the rhythms of your body taking the nourishment and nutrients into your breasts, helping them grow. The rhythm is steady, smooth, like the ticking of a clock . . . or the beating of a heart. You sense the gentle, smooth beating of your heart as it directs the blood into your breasts. You are now in tune with the rhythm of your heart. You *feel the pulsations* in your breasts, bringing the nutrients, helping them to grow. The gentle, smooth pulsation is helping your breasts to grow larger, firmer, lovelier.

Your breasts swell and grow with these gentle rhythms of your body. With each pleasant pulsation the rhythm increases the blood flow to your breasts. The gentle, consistent rhythm is causing your breasts to *grow larger and larger.* You are pleased with the sensations and you are pleased with the growth. You feel a sense of pride as your breasts are growing to lovelier, more attractive proportions.

BIO-IMAGE #6

And now as you enjoy this comfortable, enjoyable feeling, imagine now that you are seated in front of an elaborate computer that you control. The computer is located deep inside your own mind. You *see* yourself inside your mind, feeling confident and secure and in control. You are in charge of this computer. You reach forward now and press a button to direct the blood flow into the breast area. As you press the button you see in your mind a series of pipelines shifting to direct the blood flow into your breasts. You follow the direction of your blood. You feel yourself flowing with it as if you were sailing in a smooth boat gliding into your breast area. The smooth and gentle ride takes you into the breast area where you can watch and supervise the growth process.

You see the nutrients going to the cells. You watch the cells grow and expand. You sense each process as the breasts increase in size.

And now you sit back and enjoy the warm comfortable sensation of the blood circulation as it goes into the breast area. You imagine a long train carrying extra nutrients and nourishment into your breasts and as they do *you feel your breasts growing.* You *feel* them getting *larger* and *larger.* And as your breasts become *more* and *more* beautiful you *feel* a sense of pride in your new, beautiful figure. Your figure has become so much more attractive, so much more beautiful. You *feel* lovely. You feel confident, secure, and pleased about your lovely new figure.

And each day you will continue to direct the flow of blood and nutrients into the breast area as your breasts continue to grow *larger* and *larger.*

Now that you have learned to relax and your mind has helped your body to grow and develop as it should, you will remember to relax daily and employ these three *Bio-Images* daily:

Bio-Image #4 — Your breasts growing and enlarging as you enjoy the pleasant feeling of warmth from the sun shining down on you.

Bio-Image #5 — You are in tune with the rhythms of your body and you feel the gentle pulsation of blood flowing into your breasts.

and

Bio-Image #6 — You direct the computer that controls your body to send an extra flow of blood into the breast area. You feel a pleasant sense of pride in your lovely new figure.

Each day that you read or listen to this Script you will learn to feel more relaxed, more comfortable about yourself, more self-assured. You can use the words "relax now" to help you drain the tensions out of your body and to relax completely. You have learned to relax and to use the three *Bio-Images* to assist your body in performing the functions you need to develop your breasts and your figure. You can attain your goal of having a beautiful figure, one you can be proud of. Using this Program will help you to continue to relax, and help your body to function as you would wish, and help you to achieve your goal of a beautiful figure. Practice these three *Bio-Images* twice daily to help your mind and your body function as you would wish. Enjoy these practice periods for their relaxation and for the vital growth they are making it possible for you to achieve.

And now, to conclude this Script, count to five after which you will feel wide awake, happy, and refreshed.

1. Feeling good, feeling pleasant, getting up.
2. More alert, more refreshed, enthusiastic.
3. Stretching your arms and legs and your body — feeling good, feeling refreshed.
4. Eyes wide open, feeling wonderful, feeling vigorous.
5. More alert, feeling refreshed, feeling vigorous.

10

How To Use The Program and The Progress Chart

Now that you've learned the scientific basis for the Program and how it works, and how visual imagery is used in the Scripts, you are ready to begin your own personal Program. To do so just follow the simple, step-by-step instructions shown below.

INSTRUCTIONS FOR USING THE PROGRAM

1. *Review the section called "Ways of Using the Scripts" in chapter 7.*
   Determine which of the 4 ways you plan to use the Scripts:
   A. Read and reread the Scripts to yourself.
   B. Study the Scripts and learn the concepts so that you can practice them in your own mind.

    C. Have a friend read the Scripts to you.

    D. Listen to the recorded version of the Scripts.

(You may, of course, use any combination of the above methods.)

2. *Write your goals on the Progress Chart in the space provided.* You should also fill in your measurements before beginning the Program.

3. *Then, get off daily by yourself and use the appropriate Script according to the method, or methods, you have chosen.* See the Schedule For Use which follows.

4. In addition to using the full Scripts once daily during the beginning weeks, as described on the Progress Chart, *use the 2 minute visualization techniques suggested in the Scripts once or twice daily.* Please notice the difference between the two processes. *In the one case you go through the complete Script; in the other case you just mentally review the images when you have a free moment during the day.* For example, visualizing the feeling of warmth in the breast area, etc.

5. *Check off your uses of the full Script, as well as your 2 minute visualizations,* and record your measurements on the Progress Chart.

6. *If you have not yet finished reading this book, continue to do so.* A complete understanding of the method will help you to get maximum benefits from the Program. You may wish to review it on occasion, or refer to it for answers to any questions you may have.

    And that's all there is to using the Program. It's simple and enjoyable. And the potential benefits of the Program can soon be yours.

SCHEDULE FOR USE

Use the Program each day according to the schedule shown below and summarized on your Progress Chart. These few minutes a day can help you enjoy the potential results available from the method. Whether you're using the written or the recorded version of the *Bio-Imagery* Scripts, when you read or listen, get off by yourself away from distractions, relax in a comfortable chair or in bed, and just let yourself relax.

The following schedule is divided into four Basic Phases. Phase V is a suggested follow-up schedule to reinforce and strengthen the value of the total Program.

Basic Phases I - IV

PHASE I (Weeks 1-10)

Use *Bio-Imagery* Script One, The Basic Program, daily during Weeks 1-4.

In weeks 5-10 you can continue using Script One daily, or you can alternate it with Script Two, The Accelerated Program, every other day. As we discussed in chapter 7, Script Two is designed to help accelerate the learning process and enhance the effectiveness of the results. For better, faster results you can continue to alternate the use of Scripts One and Two for the balance of the Program. You'll find this schedule will add more variety to the Program and help you to keep your interest at a peak. At any time during the Program, or indeed throughout the entire Program, you can also use the Maximum Effects Script. This Script is designed to help you maximize your results, progress rapidly, and overcome "plateaus." Plan to use it once or twice weekly in place of the other Scripts, or as a helpful "extra." You'll find that this Script will not only help you with the Program, but will help you in a great many other ways as well. For a full understanding of the benefits of using this Script see chapters 13 and 14.

PHASE II (Weeks 11 & 12)
  Use the Scripts 3 times per week for 2 weeks.

PHASE III (Weeks 13 & 14)
  Use the Scripts twice weekly for 2 weeks.

PHASE IV (Weeks 15 & 16)
  Use the Scripts once weekly for 2 weeks.

Follow-Up Phase

PHASE V
  Use the Scripts on a bi-monthly basis thereafter as long as needed.

* * * * *

As you begin your figure development Program it's helpful to make effective use of the Progress Chart so that you can keep track of your progress.

The Progress Chart provides you with the complete schedule for using the *Bio-Imagery Programming* method. It has the added benefit of charting your progress as you move toward your goal. Most important of all, it provides feedback of your progress, and helps you keep on track to use the Program consistently as you progress toward your goal.

RECORDING YOUR MEASUREMENTS

As you record your measurements on your Progress Chart you'll find it helpful to indicate your cup size both before starting the Program and after it is completed.

In addition to keeping track of the measurement of your bustline, you'll find one other measurement helpful: the measurement of your chest immediately *below* your breasts. If this goes *down* as you progress on the Program it means that your breasts will appear larger in relation to your body. This is part of the proportioning effect indicated in the Williams study and explored further in the study by Staib and Logan. (The Williams study discussed the area directly below the breasts; Staib and Logan studied waist reduction also). A combination of an increase in your bustline *and* a decrease in your chest size *below* the breasts means that the *net increase in your breast size is actually larger than that indicated by just measuring your bustline.* For example, if your bust increases 2 inches and your chest measurement *immediately below* your breasts decreases 1 inch, your actual net increase would be *3* inches.

THE TWO MINUTE VISUALIZATION TECHNIQUE

The *Bio-Imagery* visualization technique that you are taught in the Scripts and on the recordings takes only 1 or 2 minutes per day. It is suggested that you use it daily both during and after the 4 Basic Phases of the programming period. It is a simple, pleasant, virtually effortless reinforcement technique that takes only a couple of minutes a day. Use the techniques suggested in the Scripts to focus your thought processes on each of the key *Bio-Images.* The *Bio-Imagery* visualization reinforces the learning program and provides additional feedback for its effective functioning. Research on learning processes has demonstrated that physiological responses *can* be controlled by thought processes. In *Bio-Imagery Programming* the purpose of the twice daily *Bio-Imagery* visualization is to reinforce the learning process, and help you to achieve the proper physiological responses. Remember too, the two essential keys to effective visualization: (1) relaxation, and (2) an intense, vivid mental image.

Be sure to check off your use of this short visualization technique in the space provided on the Progress Chart.

**YOUR
PROGRESS
CHART**

New DIMENSIONS® II BIO-IMAGERY PROGRAMMING ™

PROGRESS CHART

NUMBER OF TIMES EACH PROGRAM WAS USED

RECOMMENDED FREQUENCY OF USE

MEASUREMENTS
Before starting Program

	BUST	CHEST	WAIST	WEIGHT
	☐	☐	☐	☐

WEEK	Script One\nThe Basic Program	Script Two\nThe Accelerated Program	Self-Image Script\nThe Maximum Effects Program	VISUAL-IZATIONS*
Script 1				
1				
2				
3				
4				
Script 1 or 1 and 2				
5				
**6				
7				
8				
9				
10				
11				
12				
13				
14				
15				
16				

BASIC PHASES I - IV

PHASE I – WEEKS 1-10
Use the Scripts once daily during Weeks 1-10.

Script One: Use in Weeks 1-4.

Script Two: Alternate with Script One from Week 5 through the balance of the Program.

The Maximum Effect Script: Use once or twice weekly anytime during the Program.

PHASE II Weeks 11 & 12
3 Times Per Week

PHASE III Weeks 13 & 14
2 Times Per Week

PHASE IV Weeks 15 & 16
Once Weekly

FOLLOW-UP PHASE

PHASE V

Scientific evidence indicates that occasional, periodic repetition helps reinforce and strengthen the value of any learning program. Therefore, periodically re-using the Scripts can be helpful.

*Use the *Bio-Imagery* Visualization Technique Suggested in The Scripts Twice Daily for 1-2 Minutes through all Phases of the Program

---

HOW THE PROGRAM WAS USED — CHECK ONE (If more than one method was used, please indicate the approximate percentage of use for each method)

☐ READING THE SCRIPTS

☐ REVIEWING THE SCRIPTS FROM MEMORY

☐ HAVING SOMEONE ELSE READ THE SCRIPTS TO YOU

☐ LISTENING TO TALKING BOOK RECORDINGS

NET CHANGE

BUST INCREASE	CHEST DECREASE	WAIST DECREASE	WEIGHT DECREASE
☐	☐	☐	☐

ADD CHEST DECREASE TO YOUR BUST INCREASE

+

***TOTAL BUST INC. ☐

*** Example: If your bust increases 2 inches and your chest measurement immediately below your breasts decreases 1 inch, your Total Net Bust Increase would be 3 inches.

BUST	WAIST	WEIGHT
☐	☐	

GOALS

**6 WEEK CHECK POINT:

People differ. Some achieve their goals much more slowly and others much more quickly. If you have reached your goal at the end of 6 weeks you may proceed directly to Phase II. If, on the other hand, at the end of the 10 week Program you would like to add 1 or 2 weeks to the basic 10 week Program to maximize your potential benefits, you may do sc. The Four Phases of the Program conform to present day scientific knowledge concerning the learning process: Phase I — Basic Learning (through the *Bio-Imagery Programming* method). Phase II — Basic Reinforcement, Phase III — Over-learning, Phase IV — Generalization.

USING YOUR PROGRESS CHART:

Enter your Goals in the space provided. Then, record your measurements before starting the Program and *each week* as you progress through the Program. Weeks 1-4 use Script One daily. Beginning with Week 5 and thereafter you may either continue to use Script One, or for faster results and enchanced effectiveness, use Scripts One and Two alternately. The Maximum Effect Script may be used once or twice weekly anytime during the Program. Place a small check in the column "number of times each Program was used" each day that you use the Program and two small checks in the "visualization" column each day that you use the *Bio-Imagery* visualization technique. At the completion of the Program, record your results in the "net change" boxes at the bottom of the Chart. Then, add your "chest decrease" to your "bust increase" to figure your "total bust increase" and record it in the box provided.

STARTING ON
YOUR OWN PERSONAL PROGRAM

Now that you understand the basic fundamentals of *Bio-Imagery Programming,* and the scientific evidence on which it is based, you can begin your own personal figure development program.

As you begin, however, it's important for you to be aware of the vital role that attitude plays in your progress on the Program — and, in fact, in your successes in almost every aspect of your life.

Here are some important thoughts to keep in mind as you begin your Program.

Decide to start your new Program *now,* and EXPECT to succeed.

Get excited about your goal — be enthusiastic.

Enthusiasm generates persistance. And persistance is important in any self-improvement program.

The best self-improvement program in the world means little or nothing to the person who doesn't follow it.

So as you begin your Program decide to be persistant. Remember that people learn at different rates, and that some people respond quickly, while others may respond more slowly.

If you're serious about reaching your figure development goals you owe it to yourself to give the method a *thorough* try. You have nothing to lose by trying — and you have the potential of a lovelier figure to gain! So follow the Program completely and carefully.

Keep your goal continually before you. Focus enthusiastically and excitedly on the mental picture of your new, lovely figure. Focus on your goal and you'll help make it happen — remember that we always gravitate toward that goal that we think about most. Concentrate on the rewards of success and not on the fear of failure. When we dwell on the fear of failure we are unconsciously setting failure up as our goal.

Imagine and visualize your success in everything you do. See the results of your goal even before you have achieved it, understanding that by changing your self-image you can help yourself immensely in many aspects of your life.

As you pursue your goal on this Program it's vitally important to understand the difference between persistance and effort. Persistance means merely using the Program on a consistent basis. Effort means trying. While trying may be important in many endeavors, it can actually be a hindrance here. In *Bio-Imagery Programming* the learning process operates on a different level. You are now learning to be aware of different bodily signals. Your new training will be most effective when you literally let go . . . when you just let it happen.*

So focus your enthusiasm on your goal and on sticking with the Program.

As you do the improvements in your self-image can begin to take place.

And each time you use the Program the visualizations can become more vivid, more intense.

As you use the Program, put a value on the benefits that can be derived from it. How valuable would it be to have a lovelier, sexier figure? What could it mean to you in

---

*Elmer and Alyce Green, and other researchers as well, have cited examples of individuals who "tried" to learn control of bodily functions through biofeedback methods but were having difficulty *until they quit trying.* Then, when they had literally given up learning, they suddenly discovered that they had learned it almost automatically. Although this Program differs from biofeedback (no elaborate equipment is used to learn this Program) the same principle applies here: relax and just let it happen. Relaxation is the key to learning; "effort" is contradictory to relaxation.

terms of personal pride and self-confidence? The benefits from this Program could make it one of the most worthwhile programs you've ever used — rewards far more valuable than the few minutes a day you spend at it.

So decide to start today on your personal figure development goals.

Remember that *BIO-IMAGERY PROGRAMMING* can be your key to the figure you've always dreamed of.

The important elements are all here:

The goal . . . of a lovelier figure for you.

The evidence . . . taken from scientific studies.

The technique . . . embodied in a carefully designed Program built with the consultation of experts.

And the Program . . . designed to help you achieve your goals.

Now *is* the time to begin your personal figure enhancement program.

So start today on an exciting new Program for improving your figure *and* your self-image.

As you use the Program, continue your quest to learn as much as you can about the method. Increasing your knowledge of the Program can help you to achieve maximum results with it. You may have started the Program without reading chapters 2 through 6. If so, it is recommended that you now read these chapters which explain *Bio-Imagery Programming* and the scientific data on which it is based. Then, as you use the Program each day, you'll find that this additional material will make the method more effective as well as more meaningful.

In addition you'll find in the chapters that follow, in Parts V and VI of this book, many additional ideas and suggestions that will help you to maximize your results and enhance the effectiveness of the Program.

PART V

Improving The Effectiveness of The Program: How To Achieve Maximum Results

11

Evaluating
Your Progress

An on-going study of the results achieved by users of the Program provides vital information on its effectiveness. Copies of Progress Charts from women who have used the Program are analyzed and collated for degrees of success and for similarities and differences in trends. This continuing feedback provides helpful ideas on various aspects of the Program. What kinds of questions do women ask? Are these questions answered in the Program material? Are the explanations complete and fully understandable? How many women complete the Program? How many drop out without giving it a fair chance?

The results of the feedback on the Program are fascinating. Many women are skeptical, at first, that it can work. After all, it seems so easy. How could something so simple actually increase breast size? Results show that for those who do follow the Program to completion, the results are generally very favorable, and statistically are comparable to those achieved in the scientific studies cited in the references.

Individuals do vary, not only in their motivation to stick to a Program, but in the results they achieve. In the clinical studies referred to earlier, the results show that the highest increase was 3.54 inches. Progress Charts that have been received on the *New Dimensions* Program show many women with gains of 4½ inches and a few as high as 6 to 8 inches. We should note, however, that the results reported in the previously published studies were corroborated in clinical settings by the scientists involved, whereas the better findings reported on the *New Dimensions* Program were supplied by users of the Program who recorded their own measurements. Although scientists may cry for greater accuracy through verified measurements, the enthusiastic women who enjoy the results feel differently. And when a woman reports going from a 32A bra to a 36C, as many women have reported, it's hard to argue that she has mismeasured by 4 inches and by 2 cup sizes!

One of the most fascinating discoveries that comes from analyzing the charts is the existence of the proportioning effect referred to in chapter 10. Although all of the clinical studies measured the increases in breast size, only one examined the concurrent reduction in the size of the chest immediately *below* the breasts, and the reduction in waist size that seems to take place concomitantly. The reduction in the chest area just below the breasts indicates an even greater increase in the actual *net* size of the breasts. And the reduction in waist size is just one more added benefit that can be derived from the Program. A very high percentage of those reporting breast increases on the *New Dimensions* Program also reported a corollary decrease in waist size. An analysis of the data obtained from the Progress Charts seems to indicate that only those who really could benefit from a waist reduction actually reduced waist size — those women who already had small waistlines increased breast size without any reduction in waist·size. Interestingly enough, there seemed to be no significant relationships between either increase or decrease in weight and either breast enlargement or waist reduction — although substantial numbers of the women benefited from the proportioning effect in both the clinical study and in the *New Dimensions'* surveys. This finding — the concomitant improved body proportions and the increase in breast size — warrants further study.

Of particular interest in the use of the *New Dimensions* Program is the finding that it is totally safe. Although thousands of women have used the Program not a single adverse consequence has been reported.

Many women find it helpful to review the Progress Charts of other women who have used the Program. In the next two chapters you will find copies of Progress Charts of women with a wide variety of starting and finishing dimensions. And since different individuals respond at different rates and in varying ways, you'll see a variety of patterns of change. You will find some women who are slow starters and others who are fast starters. Women of every shape and size have used the Program.

Since the charts show waist measurements, you'll be able to note the effects of waist reduction on some of these women. Unfortunately the charts do not show the chest measurement immediately *below* the breasts so you will not be able to evaluate fully the proportioning effect on these women. Remember that decreases in chest measurement actually mean that the *net* increase in breast size is even larger than the increases shown on the charts for most of these women. The new chart that you will be using does have a place to record this additional measurement (see chapter 10). It has also been revised so that you can use it in *any* of the four ways described in chapter 7. So although the earlier version of the chart, as reproduced on the following pages, refers to the use of recordings, you should refer to chapter 7 to determine which of the four ways you plan to use the Scripts.

Look over the charts* on the pages that follow. Read the comments accompanying each chart as you study each woman's progress in order to help you interpret each chart properly.

From time to time, as you are progressing on your own personal Program, you may find it helpful to again browse through these charts.

---

*The original signed copy of all charts are on file at New Directions, Inc. To protect the privacy of the women involved no names are shown on any of the quotations or charts reproduced in this book.

As it was mentioned in chapter 1, it is important to note that although occasional reference is made to the use of recordings in earlier versions of the Program, the entire Program is now in *written* form and is contained in the pages of this book. The book itself is designed so that it can be used totally independent of any recordings. (However, Talking Book Transcripts are available for those who prefer this convenience – see chapter 7 for a discussion of ways to use the Program. No medical claims of any sort are made for the recordings.) This newly improved Program has been greatly revised and expanded and incorporates significant improvements based on extensive experience with the Program, as well as the latest research findings on the method. The newly revised Progress Chart shown in chapter 10, and the instructions for the use of the Program in chapters 7 and 10, discuss the many alternate ways in which the Program can be used. The new chart also incorporates a revised schedule of use which shows how the Accelerated and Maximum Effects Programs can be effectively utilized with the Basic Program.

SAMPLE PROGRESS CHARTS – PART 1

New DIMENSIONS™ BIO-IMAGERY PROGRAMMING™

PROGRESS CHART

			MEASUREMENTS Before starting program		
	NUMBER OF TIMES RECORDING		$31\frac{1}{2}$	24	112
WEEK	WAS PLAYED	VISUALIZATION	BUST	WAIST	WEIGHT
SIDE 1					
1	ＵＴＴ ＵＴＴ ////	ＵＴＴ ＵＴＴ	32	24	112
2	ＵＴＴ ＵＴＴ ＵＴＴ	ＵＴＴ ＵＴＴ	33	$23\frac{1}{2}$	112
3	ＵＴＴ ＵＴＴ ////	ＵＴＴ ＵＴＴ //	$33\frac{1}{2}$	24	112
4	ＵＴＴ ＵＴＴ ////	ＵＴＴ ＵＴＴ	34	23	112
5	ＵＴＴ ＵＴＴ ////	ＵＴＴ ＵＴＴ	$34\frac{1}{2}$	23	112
SIDE 2					
6	ＵＴＴ ＵＴＴ	ＵＴＴ ＵＴＴ	35	23	111
7	ＵＴＴ ＵＴＴ	ＵＴＴ ＵＴＴ	$35\frac{1}{4}$	23	111
8	ＵＴＴ //	ＵＴＴ //	$35\frac{1}{2}$	23	110
9	ＵＴＴ //	ＵＴＴ //	$35\frac{3}{4}$	23	110
10	ＵＴＴ ///	ＵＴＴ ///	36	$22\frac{1}{2}$	110
11	ＵＴＴ	ＵＴＴ	36	$22\frac{1}{2}$	111
12	ＵＴＴ	ＵＴＴ	36	$22\frac{1}{2}$	111
13	ＵＴＴ	ＵＴＴ	36	23	111
14	ＵＴＴ	ＵＴＴ	36	23	111
15	ＵＴＴ	ＵＴＴ	36	23	112
16	ＵＴＴ	ＵＴＴ	36	23	111

NET CHANGE	$4\frac{1}{2}"$	/	/LB.
	BUST INCREASE	WAIST DECREASE	WEIGHT DECREASE

S. D., CARSON CITY, NV. – A 4½" increase in bust size and a 1" decrease in waist size – excellent results. From a 31½" bust measurement to 36" is a highly significant change. And at the end of the Program she still weighed only 111 pounds. Most of S. D.'s progress came in the first 60 days on the Program.

New DIMENSIONS™ BIO-IMAGERY PROGRAMMING™

PROGRESS CHART

MEASUREMENTS
Before starting program

WEEK	NUMBER OF TIMES RECORDING WAS PLAYED	VISUALIZATION	BUST	WAIST	WEIGHT
			35$\frac{1}{2}$	25	125
SIDE 1	x x x x x x	xx xx xx xx			
1	x	xx xx xx	36	25	125
2	xxx x x x x	xx x x xx x xx	37	25	125
3	x x x x x x x	xx xx xx xx xx xx	37	25	120
4	xx xxxx x	xx xx xx xx xx xx	37	24½	120
5	xx xx x x x	xx xx xx xx xx xx	37	24	122
SIDE 2					
6	x x x x	xx xx xx xx xx xx	37	24	121
7	x x x	xx xx xx xx xx xx	37½	24	120
8	xx x	xx xx xx xx xx xx	37½	24	120
9	xxx	xx xx xx xx xx		24	120
10	xxx	xx xx xx xx xx		24	121
11	x x	xx xx xx xx xx	37½	24	119
12	x x	xx xx xx xx xx	37½	24	119
13					
14					
15					
16					

NET CHANGE	2 ½ in.	1 in.	6 lb.
	BUST INCREASE	WAIST DECREASE	WEIGHT DECREASE

M. S., SEATTLE, WA — M. S. seems to be one of the lucky fast starters. She gained 1" her very first week and another the second. By the 7th week she had gone from her original 35" to 37½", and had lost 1" in her waist and 6 pounds off her weight.

New DIMENSIONS™ BIO-IMAGERY PROGRAMMING™

PROGRESS CHART

WEEK	NUMBER OF TIMES RECORDING WAS PLAYED	VISUALIZATION	MEASUREMENTS Before starting program		
			BUST 36	WAIST 28	WEIGHT 135
SIDE 1					
1	ᵗᴴ⅃ ᵗᴴᴸ I	ᵗᴴᴸ ᵗᴴᴸ I	37	27½	135
2	ᵗᴴᴸ ᵗᴴᴸ IIII	ᵗᴴᴸ ᵗᴴᴸ IIII	37½	28	130
3	ᵗᴴᴸ ᵗᴴᴸ IIII	ᵗᴴᴸ ᵗᴴᴸ IIII	38	27½	125
4	ᵗᴴᴸ ᵗᴴᴸ IIII	ᵗᴴᴸ ᵗᴴᴸ IIII	38½	27½	124
5	ᵗᴴᴸ ᵗᴴᴸ IIII	ᵗᴴᴸ ᵗᴴᴸ IIII	38½	28	122
SIDE 2					
6	ᵗᴴᴸ ᵗᴴᴸ IIII	ᵗᴴᴸ ᵗᴴᴸ IIII	39	27	120
7	ᵗᴴᴸ ᵗᴴᴸ IIII	ᵗᴴᴸ ᵗᴴᴸ IIII	39½	26	119
8	ᵗᴴᴸ ᵗᴴᴸ IIII	ᵗᴴᴸ ᵗᴴᴸ IIII	39½	25	117
9	ᵗᴴᴸ ᵗᴴᴸ IIII	ᵗᴴᴸ ᵗᴴᴸ IIII	40	25	115
10	ᵗᴴᴸ ᵗᴴᴸ IIII	ᵗᴴᴸ ᵗᴴᴸ IIII	40	25	109
11					
12					
13					
14					
15					
16					

NET CHANGE

40	25	109
BUST INCREASE	WAIST DECREASE	WEIGHT DECREASE

J. M., FT. LAUDERDALE, FL — Another fast starter with outstanding results: 4" bust gain, 3" waist decrease, and a 26 pound weight loss. Notice her consistency in following the Program.

151

New DIMENSIONS™ BIO-IMAGERY PROGRAMMING™

PROGRESS CHART

WEEK	NUMBER OF TIMES RECORDING WAS PLAYED	VISUALIZATION	MEASUREMENTS Before starting program		
			BUST `34`	**WAIST** `29`	**WEIGHT** `135`
SIDE 1					
1	14		34	29	133
2	14		34	29	130
3	14		34	29	130
4	14		34	28	129
5	14		35	27½	128
SIDE 2					
6	14		35	27½	127
7	14		35½	27	127
8	14		36	27	126
9	14		36	26	125
10	14		36	26	125
11	7		36	26	125
12	7		36	26	125
13	7		36	26	125
14	7		36	26	125
15	4		36	26	125
16	4		36	26	125

NET CHANGE `2"` `3"` `8 lb`

| BUST INCREASE | WAIST DECREASE | WEIGHT DECREASE |

S. M., ESSEX, ONTARIO. — Here's a nice combination: a 2" bust increase, 3" waist decrease, and an 8 pound reduction in weight. Notice that she had no increase in bust size at all until the second month . . . then she made her greatest progress. More typically there will be some gains in the first 30 days. It is quite typical, however, for women to show their best gains in the second month of the Program.

New DIMENSIONS™ BIO-IMAGERY PROGRAMMING™

PROGRESS CHART

WEEK	NUMBER OF TIMES RECORDING WAS PLAYED	VISUALIZATION	MEASUREMENTS Before starting program		
			35 BUST	27 WAIST	115 WEIGHT
SIDE 1					
1	✓✓✓✓✓✓	✓✓✓✓✓✓✓✓✓✓	35½	27	115
2	ШП II	ШП ШП IIII	35½	27	115
3	ШП II	ШП ШП IIII	35¾	27	115
4	ШП II	ШП ШП IIII	36	27	115
5	ШП II	ШП ШП IIII	36	27	115
SIDE 2					
6	ШП II	ШП ШП IIII	36	27	115
7	ШП II	ШП ШП IIII	36½	27	115
8	ШП II	ШП ШП IIII	36½	26½	115
9	ШП II	ШП ШП IIII	36½	26½	115
10	ШП II	ШП ШП IIII	37	26	115
11	ШП II	ШП ШП IIII	37	26	115
12	ШП II	ШП ШП IIII	37½	26	115
13	ШП II	ШП ШП ▓	37½	26	115
14	ШП II	ШП ШП ▓	37½	26	115
15	ШП II	ШП ШП ▓	37½	26	115
16	ШП II	ШП ШП ▓	37½	26	115

NET CHANGE	2 in.	1 in.	same
	BUST INCREASE	WAIST DECREASE	WEIGHT DECREASE

T. N., SAVANNA, IL — T. N.'s progress is gradual and consistent. The fact that she was still increasing in weeks 12 - 16 indicates she might be able to achieve even more later on ... but she had reached her goal and was satisfied. Notice her consistency in using the Program which probably contributed to her steady results.

New DIMENSIONS™   BIO-IMAGERY PROGRAMMING™

PROGRESS CHART

WEEK	NUMBER OF TIMES RECORDING WAS PLAYED	VISUALIZATION	MEASUREMENTS Before starting program BUST	WAIST	WEIGHT
			32	27	132
SIDE 1					
1	1 time daily	2 times daily	32	27	132
2	//	//	32	27	132
3	//	//	32	27	132
4	//	//	32	27	131
5	//	//	34	26	130
SIDE 2					
6	//	//	34	26	130
7	//	//	34	26	130
8	//	//	34	26	128
9	//	//	35	26	127
10	//	//	35	26	127
11	//	//	35	25	127
12	//	//	35	25	125
13	//	//	35	25	125
14	//	//	35	24	124
15	//	//	36	24	120
16	/	//	36	24	120

NET CHANGE 4 inches   3 inches   12 lbs

BUST INCREASE   WAIST DECREASE   WEIGHT DECREASE

L. R., SYRACUSE, NY — L. C. was one of many skeptics who had failed to get results with a string of exercisers, proteins, etc. — but look at her results with this Program! 4" bust increase, 3" waist decrease, and 12 pounds off her weight. No wonder she calls herself the "new me".

New DIMENSIONS™ BIO-IMAGERY PROGRAMMING™

PROGRESS CHART

WEEK	NUMBER OF TIMES RECORDING WAS PLAYED	VISUALIZATION	MEASUREMENTS BUST	WAIST	WEIGHT
Before starting program			35½	26½	120lbs
SIDE 1					
1	7	14	35½	26½	120lbs
2	7	13	35¾	26½	118lbs
3	7	15	35¾	25¼	114lbs
4	7	12	36	25¼	114lbs
5	7	14	36¼	25¼	114lbs
SIDE 2					
6	3	12	36	25¼	112lbs
7	3	14	36½	25¼	112lbs
8	3	13	36½	25	110lb
9	3	14	36½	25	110lb
10	3	15	37	25	110 lbs
11	2	14	37	25	111 lbs
12	2	10	37½	25	110½ ½
13	2	11	37½	25	110lbs
14	2	14	37¾	25	111 lbs.
15	2	12	37¾	25	110lbs
16	2	11	37¾	25	110½lbs.
NET CHANGE			2¼ BUST INCREASE	1½ WAIST DECREASE	10lbs. WEIGHT DECREASE

E. S., MIAMI, FL – Bust size up 2¼", waist size down 1½". And it's nice to lose 10 pounds when you're overweight. Consistent use here results in consistent progress.

New DIMENSIONS™ BIO-IMAGERY PROGRAMMING™

PROGRESS CHART

WEEK	NUMBER OF TIMES RECORDING WAS PLAYED	VISUALIZATION	MEASUREMENTS Before starting program		
			35	27	121
			BUST	WAIST	WEIGHT
SIDE 1					
1	14	10	35¼	26¾	121
2	10	4	35½	26½	120
3	8	8	35½	26½	119
4	4	8	35⅝	26½	119
5	7	8	36	26½	120
SIDE 2					
6	7	6	36	26½	119
7	5	8	36¼	26½	121
8	7	7	36½	26½	119
9	6	5	36½	26½	121
10	2	5	36⅞	26½	122
11	7	7	36⅝	26½	122
12	7	9	36⅞	26½	122
13	6	6	36⅞	26½	122
14	8	3	37⅛	26½	121
15					
16					

NET CHANGE

2⅛"	1½"	0
BUST INCREASE	WAIST DECREASE	WEIGHT DECREASE

P. P., NACOGDOCHES, TX — From 35" to 37-1/8". No wonder she said that her "boyfriend sure was surprised." She enjoyed nice consistent progress right through the 14th week.

New DIMENSIONS™ BIO-IMAGERY PROGRAMMING™

PROGRESS CHART

			MEASUREMENTS Before starting program		
			36	31	131
WEEK	NUMBER OF TIMES RECORDING WAS PLAYED	VISUALIZATION	BUST	WAIST	WEIGHT
SIDE 1					
1	12 times	12 times	36	30	131
2	12 times	" "	36½"	30	130
3	12 "	" "	37	29	130
4	12 "	" "	37½	29	129
5	12 "	" "	38	29	129
SIDE 2					
6	12 "	" "	38¼	29	129
7	12 "	" "	38½	29	129
8	12 "	" "	38½	28	129
9	12 "	" "	38½	28	128
10	12 "	" "	38½	28	128
11	12 "	" "	38½	28	128
12	12 "	" "	38½	28	128
13					
14					
15					
16					

NET CHANGE	2½ inch	4 inch	3 pds
	BUST INCREASE	WAIST DECREASE	WEIGHT DECREASE

V. T., MURRAY, UT — A 2" increase in bust size in the first 5 weeks means it was easy going for V. T. For some people it just seems easier to learn to relax, and to learn to use the method. And for some people, for many reasons, the self-image may be more ready for a change. Not much weight change here, but she did benefit from a 4" decrease in waist size and enjoyed a total bust increase of 2½".

New DIMENSIONS™ BIO-IMAGERY PROGRAMMING™

PROGRESS CHART

WEEK	NUMBER OF TIMES RECORDING WAS PLAYED	VISUALIZATION	MEASUREMENTS Before starting program		
			BUST 32	WAIST 25	WEIGHT 112
SIDE 1		√√ √√			
1	√ √√√ √√	√√√ √√√√√	32	25	112
2	√√√√ √√	√√√√ √√√√√√√√	32½	25	112
3	√√√√√√	√√√√√√√√√√√	32½	25	112
4	√√√√√√	√√√√√√√√√√	33	25	111
5	√√√√√√√	√√√√√√√√√√	33	25	111
SIDE 2					
6	√√√√√√	√√√√√√√√√√√	33½	24½	109
7	√√√√√√√	√√√√√√√√√√	33½	24½	109
8	√√√√√√√	√√√√√√√√√√	34	24	107
9	√√√√√√√	√√√√√√√√√√	34	24	107
10	√√√√√√√	√√√√√√√√√√	34	24	106
11	√√√√√√√√	√√√√√√√√√√√	34	24	105
12	√√√√ √√√√	√√√√√√√√√√√	34	24	105
13					
14					
15					
16					

NET CHANGE	2 inches	1 inch	7 lb
	BUST INCREASE	WAIST DECREASE	WEIGHT DECREASE

P. W., GREELY, CO — P. W. benefited from gradual and consistent change. Her shape certainly has better proportions as she changed from 32-25 to 34-24 in bust and waist measurements, respectively. If she wishes to gain more she might benefit from returning to the Program after 2 or 3 months.

New DIMENSIONS™ BIO-IMAGERY PROGRAMMING™

PROGRESS CHART

WEEK	NUMBER OF TIMES RECORDING WAS PLAYED	VISUALIZATION	MEASUREMENTS Before starting program		
			BUST 35	WAIST 27	WEIGHT 130
SIDE 1					
1	7		35	26½	130
2	7		35½	26½	"
3	12		"	"	"
4	12		36	"	"
5	12		"	"	"
SIDE 2					
6	7		37	25½	125
7	7		38	"	"
8	7		"	"	"
9	7		"	"	122
10	7		"	"	"
11	7		38¼	25"	"
12	7		"	25"	120
13					
14					
15					
16					

NET CHANGE	3¼" BUST INCREASE	2" WAIST DECREASE	10 lbs WEIGHT DECREASE

J. W., NEWARF, DE — Nice results here. 3¼" bust increase. 2" waist decrease, and a 10 pound weight loss. It's easy to be pleased with results like this — especially when they are fairly consistent throughout the Program as they were in the first 2 months for J. W.

New DIMENSIONS™ BIO-IMAGERY PROGRAMMING™

PROGRESS CHART

WEEK	NUMBER OF TIMES RECORDING WAS PLAYED	VISUALIZATION	MEASUREMENTS Before starting program		
			32A BUST	29" WAIST	120 lbs WEIGHT
SIDE 1					
1	*Ⅱ ⅡⅡ ⅡⅡ ⅡⅡ Ⅱ ⅥⅠ*	*ⅡⅡⅡⅡⅡ Ⅱ ⅡⅡ*	32½	28½"	120 lbs
2	*Ⅱ ⅡⅡ ⅡⅡⅡ ⅡⅥ*	*ⅡⅡ ⅡⅡⅡ ⅡⅡⅡ*	33 "	28"	120 lbs
3	*ⅡⅡ ⅡⅡ ⅡⅡ ⅡⅡ*	*ⅡⅡⅡⅡ AⅡ*	34 "	26½ "	115 lbs
4	*ⅡⅡⅡⅡ ⅡⅡ Ⅱ*	*ⅡⅡ ⅡA Ⅱ ⅡⅡ*	3 5 "	26 "	115 lbs
5	*ⅡⅡ Ⅱ ⅡⅡ Ⅱ Ⅱ Ⅱ*	*ⅡⅡⅡ ⅡⅡ Ⅱ Ⅱ*	35½	26 "	115 lbs
SIDE 2					
6	*Ⅱ ⅡⅡ ⅡⅡⅡ Ⅱ*		36"	26 "	115 lbs
7	*ⅡⅡ ⅡⅡⅡⅡⅡ*	*ⅡⅡⅡ ⅡⅡⅡⅡ*	36"	26 "	115 lbs
8	*Ⅱ ⅡⅡⅡ Ⅱ ⅡⅡ*	*Ⅱ ⅡⅡ A Ⅱ Ⅱ*	36 "	26 "	115 lbs
9	*Ⅱ Ⅱ ⅡⅡ Ⅱ ⅡⅡ*	*Ⅱ ⅡⅡ ⅡⅡⅡ Ⅱ*	36 "	26 "	115 lbs
10	*ⅡⅡⅡⅡ ⅡⅡⅡ Ⅱ*	*ⅡⅡⅡ ⅡⅡⅡ Ⅱ*	36½"	26 "	115 lbs
11	*Ⅱ ⅡⅡ Ⅱ A ⅡⅡⅡ*	*ⅡⅡ Ⅱ ⅡⅡ Ⅱ*	36½ "	26 "	115 lbs
12	*Ⅱ ⅡⅡⅡ Ⅱ Ⅱ ⅡⅡ*	*ⅡⅡ Ⅱ A ⅡⅡ*	36½ "	26 "	115 lbs
13					
14					
15					
16					

NET CHANGE

36½" BUST INCREASE	26" WAIST DECREASE	115 lbs WEIGHT DECREASE

K. T., SALT LAKE CITY, UT — After 3 children K. W. was
delighted to go from 32" to 36½", take 3" off her waist and find
that her scales registered a 5 pound weight decrease. From her chart
we see that she actually used the Script more than was necessary —
but her results show that she used her time wisely.

12

Learning
From Others

Periodically you may have questions about your individual rate of response to the Program. Are you a fast-starter or a slow starter? How do you overcome a plateau (i.e. a period in which there is no obvious growth)? Does a plateau mean that you can't go any farther? (You'll find more information on these topics in chapters 13 and 14.) How does cup size enter into the measuring procedure?

. The Progress Charts on the following pages will help you answer these questions. Study the charts and read the comments. You'll find the answers reassuring. These women, in spite of plateaus, and in spite of widely varying rates of response, all benefited from the Program. Their charts can be of help to you as you progress towards your goal. Some of these women may have had the same feelings you have had . . . and perhaps similar reasons for exploring this breast enlargement method. Some had the same doubts, the same distractions, the same reasons for procrastinating, as you may have. But they faced these problems and went on to benefit from the Program. If they did it, you can too!

The message from these Progress Charts is clear: It works. It's easy. It's relaxing. It's fun. And the payoff of a lovelier figure and a better self-image are the delightful rewards of the Program.

SAMPLE PROGRESS CHARTS – PART 2

New DIMENSIONS™ BIO-IMAGERY PROGRAMMING™

PROGRESS CHART

WEEK	NUMBER OF TIMES RECORDING WAS PLAYED	VISUALIZATION	MEASUREMENTS Before starting program BUST [36]	WAIST [28]	WEIGHT [130]
SIDE 1					
1	✓✓✓✓✓✓✓	wwwww/ wwwj	36	27½	130
2	✓✓✓✓✓✓	wwwwwjw	36¼	27	132
3	✓✓✓✓✓✓	wwwwwww	36½	26½	131
4	✓✓✓✓✓✓	wwwwwww	36½	26½	130
5	✓✓✓✓✓✓	wwwwwww	36¾	26	129
SIDE 2					
6	✓✓✓✓✓✓	╫╫╫╫╫	37¾	26	128
7	✓✓✓✓✓✓	╫╫╫╫╫	38	26	128
8	✓✓✓✓✓✓	╫╫╫╫╫	38¼	26	127
9	✓✓✓✓✓✓	╫╫╫╫╫	38¾	26¼	127
10	✓✓✓✓✓✓	╫╫╫╫╫	39½	26	126
11	✓✓✓✓	╫╫╫╫╫	38¾	26	126
12	✓✓✓	╫╫╫╫╫	39	26	126
13					
14					
15					
16					

NET CHANGE

☐	☐	☐
BUST INCREASE	WAIST DECREASE	WEIGHT DECREASE

L. C., BALTIMORE, MD – L. C. had good reason to be so pleased with her results: bust increase 3", waist decrease 2". Notice here that most of her gains did not take place until the 6th week. It was worth sticking with the Program for the 12 weeks.

New DIMENSIONS™   BIO-IMAGERY PROGRAMMING™

PROGRESS CHART

WEEK	NUMBER OF TIMES RECORDING WAS PLAYED	VISUALIZATION	MEASUREMENTS Before starting program 32A BUST	28 WAIST	135 WEIGHT
SIDE 1					
1	2	``	32A	28	135
2	2	``	32½	28	132
3	2	``	33	27½	130
4	2	``	34	27	129
5	2	``	34B	26	125
SIDE 2					
6	2	``	34B	26	120
7	2	``	``	``	``
8	2	``	``	``	``
9	2	``	``	``	``
10	2	``	``	``	``
11	2	``	``		
12	2	``	``	``	
13	2	``	``	``	``
14	2	``	``	``	``
15	2	``	``		``
16	2	``	``	``	``

NET CHANGE

2 sizes BUST INCREASE	2 WAIST DECREASE	15 WEIGHT DECREASE

B. W., VALPARAISO, IN — From 32A to 34B — good measurement and good cup size increases. Since she also lost 15 pounds and 2 inches from her waistline it's easy to see why she was so pleased with the Program. And it's always a source of fascination to marvel at the awesome effectiveness of the technique when it is actually able to increase breast size in spite of significant reduction in weight. Note that B. W. is one of the lucky women who are truly fast starters — she reached her goal in just 5 weeks.

New DIMENSIONS™ BIO-IMAGERY PROGRAMMING™

PROGRESS CHART

WEEK	NUMBER OF TIMES RECORDING WAS PLAYED	VISUALIZATION	MEASUREMENTS Before starting program		
			BUST	WAIST	WEIGHT
			32	*27*	*113*
SIDE 1					
1	4	4	32	27	113
2	8	4	32	27	112
3	4	5	32½	27	113
4	7	4	32½	27	113
5	6	4	32½	26	111
SIDE 2					
6	4	4	33	26	111
7	7	8	33	26	111
8	8	8	33	26	110
9	9	7	33	26	110
10	7	4	33	26	111
11	9	9	33½	26	110
12	9	9	33½	26	110
13	9	9	34	26	110
14	9	9	34	26	110
15	9	9	35	26	110
16	9	9	35	26	110

NET CHANGE	3″	1″	3#
	BUST INCREASE	WAIST DECREASE	WEIGHT DECREASE

L. S., EPHRATA, PA — Here is an excellent example of the plateau that many women face . . . and the value of persisting through those slow periods. It took her 6 weeks to gain 1" and she then leveled off and made no visable progress from weeks 6 - 10. If she had quit at the end of week 10 she would have assumed that she had gone as far as she could. Fortunately she did persist and in weeks 11 - 16 increased 2 additional inches. The lesson? Even though visable progress is not being made, it doesn't mean that you are not progressing. Remember that the Program is continually working to improve your self-image . . . and that image can be exceedingly stubborn at times in accepting a change. Then, suddenly, as may have happened here, a breakthrough is made which allows you to move forward as the factors inhibiting breast growth are broken down (see chapters 13 and 14).

New DIMENSIONS™ BIO-IMAGERY PROGRAMMING™

PROGRESS CHART

MEASUREMENTS
Before starting program

WEEK	NUMBER OF TIMES RECORDING WAS PLAYED	VISUALIZATION	35 BUST	28½ WAIST	142 WEIGHT
SIDE 1					
1	7	14	35	28½	142
2	7	14	35	28½	140
3	7	14	35	28	140
4	7	14	35½	28	140
5	7	14	35½	28	140
SIDE 2					
6	7	14	36	28	143
7	7	14	36	27½	143
8	7	14	36	27½	143
9	7	14	36½	27½	144
10	7	14	36½	27½	144
11	7	14	37	27½	145
12	7	14	37	27½	145
13	7	14	37	27½	146
14	7	14	37½	27½	148
15	7	14	37½	27	148
16	7	14	38	27	148

NET CHANGE 3 in — BUST INCREASE   2½ in. — WAIST DECREASE   ✓ — WEIGHT DECREASE

C. C., SALT LAKE CITY, UT – C. C. is another woman who could easily have quit at the end of 12 weeks. But persisting for 4 more weeks paid off with the gain of another inch, bringing her total to 3". No weight loss here, but she did reduce her waistline by 2½".

New DIMENSIONS™ BIO-IMAGERY PROGRAMMING™

PROGRESS CHART

WEEK	NUMBER OF TIMES RECORDING WAS PLAYED	VISUALIZATION	MEASUREMENTS Before starting program BUST	WAIST	WEIGHT
			32	22	117
SIDE 1					
1	7	13	33	22	117
2	6	14	33		117
3	7		33½		117
4	7	)	33½		116
5	5	(	34		115
SIDE 2					
6	5	12	34	22	115
7	6	13	34	22	
8	6	13	34½	21½	
9	7	14	35	21½	
10	7	14	35	21½	
11	5	10	35	21½	115
12	4	10	35		115
13	3	12	35		115
14	3	10	35		115
15	3	13	35½		114
16	4	14	35½		114

NET CHANGE: 3½ in — BUST INCREASE | ½ in — WAIST DECREASE | 3 lb — WEIGHT DECREASE

K. O., LEBANON, MO — No significant change in waist size here, but how about that 3½" increase in bust size! No wonder she reports feeling better about herself and a new sense of pride in herself. It's nice to increase bust size but the real benefit is the improved self-image!

New DIMENSIONS™   BIO-IMAGERY PROGRAMMING™

PROGRESS CHART

MEASUREMENTS
Before starting program

WEEK	NUMBER OF TIMES RECORDING WAS PLAYED	VISUALIZATION	BUST **33**	WAIST **26**	WEIGHT **105**
SIDE 1					
1	𝍩𝍩 //	𝍩𝍩 𝍩𝍩 ////	33½	26	105
2	𝍩𝍩 //	𝍩𝍩 𝍩𝍩 ////	35	26	105
3	𝍩𝍩 //	𝍩𝍩 𝍩𝍩 ////	35	26	105
4	𝍩𝍩 //	𝍩𝍩 𝍩𝍩 ///	35	26	107
5	𝍩𝍩 //	𝍩𝍩 𝍩𝍩 ////	35½	26	105
SIDE 2					
6	𝍩𝍩 //	𝍩𝍩 𝍩𝍩 ////	35½	26	105
7	𝍩𝍩 //	𝍩𝍩 𝍩𝍩 ////	35½	26	105
8	𝍩𝍩 //	𝍩𝍩 𝍩𝍩 ////	35½	26	106
9	𝍩𝍩 //	𝍩𝍩 𝍩𝍩 ////	35½	26	106
10	𝍩𝍩 //	𝍩𝍩 𝍩𝍩 ////	35½	26	106
11	𝍩𝍩 //	𝍩𝍩 𝍩𝍩 ////	36	26	107
12	𝍩𝍩 //	𝍩𝍩 𝍩𝍩 ////	36	26	105
13	𝍩𝍩 //	𝍩𝍩 𝍩𝍩 ///	36	26	105
14	𝍩𝍩 //	𝍩𝍩 𝍩𝍩 ///	36	26	105
15	𝍩𝍩 /	𝍩𝍩 𝍩𝍩 //	36	26	105
16	𝍩𝍩 //	𝍩𝍩 𝍩𝍩 //	36	26	106

NET CHANGE	**3 inches**	**none**	**none**
	BUST INCREASE	WAIST DECREASE	WEIGHT DECREASE

G. S., KANSAS CITY, MO — No waist change here either. But with her 3" bust increase she's now 36-26. Sounds like a good balance.

New DIMENSIONS™ BIO-IMAGERY PROGRAMMING™

PROGRESS CHART

WEEK	NUMBER OF TIMES RECORDING WAS PLAYED	VISUALIZATION	MEASUREMENTS Before starting program		
			31	27	120
			BUST	WAIST	WEIGHT
SIDE 1					
1	7	7	32	27	120
2	14	14	32	27	120
3	21	25	32,5	27	120
4	28	35	33	27	120
5	35	42	33,5	27	121
SIDE 2					
6	42	49	34	27,5	122
7	49	56	34	27,5	122
8	56	63	34,5	27,5	122
9	63	70	35	27	122
10	77	84	35,5	27	122
11	7	20	36	27	122
12	7	20	36,5	27	122
13					
14					
15					
16					

NET CHANGE	4,5	—	—
	BUST INCREASE	WAIST DECREASE	WEIGHT DECREASE

R. S., BROOKLYN, NY — R. S. is one of the women without a change in waist size. But her 4½" increase in bust size makes it all worthwhile.

New DIMENSIONS™   BIO-IMAGERY PROGRAMMING™

PROGRESS CHART

WEEK	NUMBER OF TIMES RECORDING WAS PLAYED	VISUALIZATION	MEASUREMENTS Before starting program		
			33 BUST	**26** WAIST	**130** WEIGHT
SIDE 1					
1	5		"	"	"
2	5.5		"	"	"
3	6		33.2	25.6	129
4	5		"	"	"
5	5		33.4	25.5	128.5
SIDE 2					
6	5	x	33.5	25.5	128
7	6	X	"	"	"
8	7	X	"	"	"
9	4	X	33.7	25.6	126
10	3.5	X	33.8	"	125
11	5	X	34	25.4	124
12	6	X	34.2	25.1	123
13	7	X	34.3	24.7	123
14	5	X	34.3	24.5	122
15	6	X	34.6	24.3	121
16	6	X	35	24.1	120

NET CHANGE	**2** BUST INCREASE	**2** WAIST DECREASE	**10 lb.** WEIGHT DECREASE

L. B., ALTADENA, CA — Here is another case of slow progress ... but by the end of the 16th week she had enjoyed a 2" bust increase, a 2" waist decrease, and a 10 lb. loss in weight. Persistence does pay off.

New DIMENSIONS™ BIO-IMAGERY PROGRAMMING™

PROGRESS CHART

MEASUREMENTS
Before starting program

WEEK	NUMBER OF TIMES RECORDING WAS PLAYED	VISUALIZATION	BUST `34`	WAIST `25½`	WEIGHT `125`
SIDE 1					
1	||||	twice per day	34	25½	125
2	|||||	once per day	34	25½	125
3	||||	once per day	34	25½	125
4	||||	twice per day	34	25	155
5	||||	twice per day	34	25	125
SIDE 2			*notice better cleavage*		
6	||||||	twice per day	34	25	125
7	||||	once per day	34½	25	125
8	||||	once per day	34½	25	125
9	||||	once per day	34½	25	125
10	|||||	once per day	34½	25	125
		breasts evening up; firmer			
11	||||	once per day	35	25	125
12	|||||	once per day	35	25	125
13					
14					
15					
16					

NET CHANGE	~~½~~ 1 in.	½ in.	—
	BUST INCREASE	WAIST DECREASE	WEIGHT DECREASE

E. P., LISLE, IL — E. P. seems pleased with her increase
Apparently the unevenness in the size of her breasts is correcting
itself. Some women feel a need for increases in the fullness in the
upper part of the breast above the nipple, for some it might be a
reduction in sagging, or for others, as in this case, more evenness in
the size of the breasts. In your visualizations, focus on the specific
benefits you wish to achieve. Two things could help here: being sure
that the 2 minute visualization is used twice each day instead of
once, and, using the Program beyond 12 weeks (or going back to it
after a couple of months.)

New DIMENSIONS™ BIO-IMAGERY PROGRAMMING™

PROGRESS CHART

			MEASUREMENTS Before starting program		
WEEK	NUMBER OF TIMES RECORDING WAS PLAYED	VISUALIZATION	34 B BUST	26 WAIST	117½ WEIGHT
SIDE 1					
1	5	10	34 B	26	117
2	7	14	34 B	25	117
3	7	14	34 B	25	117
4	7	14	34 B	25	116
5	7	14	34 C	25	116
SIDE 2					
6	6	11	34 C	25	115
7	7	14	34 C	25	115 ½
8	7	14	34 C	24	115
9	7	14	34 C	24	115
10	7	14	34 C	24	114
11	5	10	34 C	24	112
12	3	6	34 C	23	110
13	3	6	34 C	23	110
14	3	6	34 C	23	110
15	3	5	34 C	23	109
16	3	5	34 C	23	109

NET CHANGE	1 full cup size	3 in	8½ lbs.
	BUST INCREASE	WAIST DECREASE	WEIGHT DECREASE

S. S., LAREDO, TX — This chart shows the value of keeping track of your cup size. Different women wish to fill in their breast size in different ways. For S. S. it was cup size. Although she started and ended with a 34" bustline, she actually went from a "B" to a "C" cup size. How did she feel about this? Her comment was . . . "talk about *curves!* Raquel Welch eat your *heart out!* Thanks for a wonderful program!" Note the 3" waist decrease she enjoyed as well.

New DIMENSIONS™   BIO-IMAGERY PROGRAMMING™

PROGRESS CHART

WEEK	NUMBER OF TIMES RECORDING WAS PLAYED	VISUALIZATION	MEASUREMENTS Before starting program $\boxed{34A}$ BUST	$\boxed{30 \, in.}$ WAIST	$\boxed{135}$ WEIGHT
SIDE 1 1	7 times/wk		34 A	30	135
2	" " / "		" "	" "	" "
3	14 times "		" "	" "	138
4	" " "		" "	" "	132
5	" " "		" "	29	" "
SIDE 2 6	7 times/wk		34 B	" "	130
7	" " / "		" "	" "	128
8	14 " "		" "	" "	" "
9	" " "		" "	" "	126
10	" " "		" "	27	" "
to 1+2 11	17 times/wk		" "	" "	125
12	" " "		" "	" "	122
13					
14					
15					
16					

NET CHANGE	1 cup	3 inches	10 pds.
	BUST INCREASE	WAIST DECREASE	WEIGHT DECREASE

W. M., PAUST, RI — Her bra size is up one full cup size and she has a smaller waistline (3 inches) and a loss in weight (10 pounds). She reports that she had tried to lose weight in the past but had been unsuccessful — but on this Program she lost it automatically.

New DIMENSIONS™   BIO-IMAGERY PROGRAMMING™

PROGRESS CHART

WEEK	NUMBER OF TIMES RECORDING WAS PLAYED	VISUALIZATION	MEASUREMENTS Before starting program 36B BUST	34 WAIST	168 WEIGHT
SIDE 1					
1	7	7	36½	34	168
2	7	7	36½	34	163
3	7	7	37	33½	163
4	7	7	37	33	162½
5	7	7	37½	32	162
SIDE 2					
6	7	7	38		
7	7	7	38	32	162½
8	7	7	39	31½	162
9	7	7	39½	31	159
10	7	7	40 C	31	158
11	7	7	40½		158
12	7	7	41¼	31½	157
13	5	5	41½	31¼	157½
14	5	5	42	29	157½
15	4	4	42	29	156
16	4	4	42 C	29	156

NET CHANGE	6" BUST INCREASE	5" WAIST DECREASE	12 WEIGHT DECREASE

M. R., ONSET, MA — M. R. is delighted with her results. A full 6" bust increase — from a 36B to a 42C. Couple this with a 5" waist decrease and a 12 pound loss in weight! No wonder she says "Bio-Imagery really works."

13

Maximizing Your Results

Our analysis of the progress of women who have followed the Program makes one thing abundantly clear: every woman is unique, progresses at her own rate, and in her own pattern of change. The probable reasons for this finding are complex. And certainly all of them are not known. Studies of how people learn, and how they relearn, provide insight into some of the factors which influence the learning process.

HOW THE SELF-IMAGE
AFFECTS YOUR PROGRESS

It seems evident that the self-image plays a vital role in the learning processes involved in *Bio-Imagery Program-*

ming. One woman who used the Program phrased it this way:

> *"I have not answered your request for comments yet because of my dropping the program for a time — as soon as the program began to work, and it does work, I dropped it. I had to come to terms with my fears about being more attractive, and I think I have. You know, you might mention to your subscribers that if the program begins to work and they conveniently find a way to stop playing the tape, the cause may be the one I mentioned."*
>
> *B.M., Austin, TX*

Her comments indicated that somehow she recognized that how a woman perceives herself and feels about her appearance — her self-image, can inhibit her success or inhibit her consistency in following the Program. Letters from other women indicate that they quite frequently find "reasons" for getting sidetracked from the Program for a period of time:

> *"I received your letter today and I am sorry to say that I haven't been using the Program lately as I should. I have been traveling and doing things that have kept me from it. However, I hope to start again very soon from the beginning. I believe that it was helping when I first started the program, therefore, I am very anxious to begin again. I was also encouraged by your letter by the fact that you are taking a special interest in the results of the program . . ."*
>
> *J.L.*

"You requested a reply as to my progress. I started the program quite regularly but got sidetracked and was not able to keep on a regular routine. When I started the program I saw results. My breasts were becoming firmer and I was very enthusiastic. I intend to start again . . ."

G. C., Los Gatos, CA

While circumstances may have played a role in causing these women to become sidetracked, it's quite possible that other factors contributed to their discontinuing the Program — especially since it seemed to be working for them.

This chapter explores some of the factors which influenced the progress of women who have used the Program. An awareness of these factors can help you to understand why some women seem to be fast starters and others are slow starters. It can also help you to analyze and overcome "plateaus."

GETTING YOUR SELF-IMAGE
TO HELP YOU SUCCEED

As we have seen the self-image plays an enormously important role in the *Bio-Imagery Programming* process. Everything that you can do to help enhance your self-image can help you to progress more effectively with the Program. That is why the technique of visualization can be helpful. We, therefore, suggest that during the day you focus on the specific concepts you learned from the Scripts regarding the visualizations and reinforce the image of yourself that you wish to attain. Picture vividly the new self-image of your attractive, lovely figure. Create your own visualizations of leaving your old self-image behind. See yourself walking away from it. Your old self-concept will begin to change as you get closer and closer to your new, improved self-image. And let go of your skepticism. Believe that you can succeed. And *know* that the Program works.

Find other ways to reinforce your new improved self-image. Keep in mind that your self-image is a central factor that helps you to move forward quickly. Most importantly, use the Scripts consistently. Remember that they were designed by an internationally-known consulting psychologist and that the learning procedures that they incorporate are designed to help you enhance your self-image as you use the Program. You may also wish to use a technique for reinforcing your new improved self-image that has been suggested by one of the researchers on the method: find a picture of a woman with the kind of figure you would like to have and paste over the picture a picture of your own face[1]. From time to time look at this picture as you are visualizing the progress you are making towards your goal.

As you are progressing toward your goal it is also helpful to understand some of the factors which may have inhibited the development of your breasts during your adolescent years. Packard points out that many of the women that she worked with in her study reported feeling a sense of anxiety, and perhaps undue concern, about the development of their own breasts during their developmental stages[1]. Le Cron also reports a similar finding[2]. In our culture, with its emphasis on youth and beauty, this kind of anxiety is not uncommon, and it could be a contributing factor in inhibiting the normal development of the breasts during the developmental stages of a young girl's life. This type of anxiety may help account for the fact that psychologists have reported case studies in which women enjoyed a natural increase in breast size following psychotherapy[3].

HOW TO ENHANCE THE EFFECTIVENESS OF THE PROGRAM

To maximize your success as you begin the Program, keep in mind these three important facts:

1. Thousands of people have learned the procedures involved in controlling blood flow for a variety of different purposes.
2. In applying these learning procedures to breast enlargement it's clear that women of every shape, size, and description have learned to enlarge their breasts.
3. By following appropriate procedures virtually all women can learn to use this method effectively.

What are the appropriate procedures? One essential factor is being *ready* to learn. The only thing that can hold you back is the rigidity of your own self-image. A deeply etched self-image can erect subconsciously oriented inhibitions in the learning pathways. At times it seems that the self-image can provide a passive oppositional aura which acts as a barrier that creates slow starters, causes plateaus, and precipitates other difficulties which interfere with the desired results.

This underscores the importance of Scripts that are designed under the direction of a knowledgeable psychologist. As you use your Scripts you will notice the careful emphasis placed on being proud of your figure and in feeling good about yourself. All of the terminology throughout the Scripts has been carefully selected to help break through any barriers that might be caused by a poor self-image — and in fact are designed to help you enhance your own self-image. It is important to understand that you cannot exceed the limits set by your own self-image. *However, you can improve your self-image and in effect adjust the limits upward.*

It is no accident that because the self-image plays such a vital role in this Program that so many women report improvements in many other aspects of their lives. In the clinical studies which we have cited, researchers report such diverse benefits as women feeling better about themselves, getting better golf and bowling scores, and feeling happier in many other aspects of their lives. These changes seem to be a direct result of the improvement in self-image that takes place with the breast enlargement that occurs.

As you progress on your personal Program there are a number of things that you can do to help enhance the effectiveness of the results. For one thing, as we have mentioned, you can work on improving your self-image in many other ways. For example, you can use the visualization techniques throughout your day — as you are walking, standing, sitting, working, etc. Another thing you can do to help is to learn more about the self-image itself. A popular and enjoyable book that you may enjoy reading is *Psychocybernetics* by Maxwell Maltz (N.Y., Simon & Schuster, 1960).

HOW TO OVERCOME PLATEAUS

Your understanding of the role of the self-image in your life can be a great help to you if you should reach a plateau on the Program, or are having trouble making a breakthrough. Understand that in all likelihood a setback is nothing more than a temporary barrier. Refer back to the Progress Charts in chapters 11 and 12 and you'll see that many women occasionally run into a temporary plateau. But you, like they, can continue to progress by continuing with the Program.

If you should reach a plateau you may find it helpful to think about some of the reasons *why* your subconscious mind may be erecting these temporary barriers. Ask yourself these questions:

1. Do you *really* want to be a lovelier woman?
2. Or, if there is something holding you back, what is it?
3. Do you recall ever having been told that you are not pretty?
4. Do you remember learning at some point in your life that you should not feel too proud of yourself?
5. Do you in some way feel that it's bad to think about having larger breasts — or did you ever get this impression through the words or actions of others when you were growing up?
6. Do you remember feeling anxious or concerned about the development of your figure when you were younger?
7. What other shackles from your past could be holding you back?
8. Are you afraid to be more attractive because you fear being with the opposite sex?

Look at some of the other aspects of your life. For example:

1. Have you gone on diets in the past but never quite succeeded?
2. Have you started exercise programs and then

dropped them?

3. Have you always wanted to have a "makeover", but have never gotten around to it?
4. Have you thought about taking self-improvement classes, but have never done it?
5. Have you wanted to wear more glamorous, more flattering clothes but have found yourself always sticking to older styles and more conservative apparel?
6. Did you start the *New Dimensions* Program but then get "too busy" to complete it?
7. Do you think well of yourself — or are you always putting yourself down, criticizing yourself continually?

In each case, the answers to these questions are, to a large measure, controlled by your self-image. If you find that you haven't done many of the things you would like to do, or find that you have neglected striving for goals you would really like to achieve, look to your self-image as one of the keys to the inhibiting factors holding you back. Then, *set up a specific plan to improve and enhance that self-image.*

HOW TO ELIMINATE PROCRASTINATION

Another technique that you can use to help clarify in your own mind some of the factors that may cause you to delay using the Program is to analyze any possible fears or traits that may be holding you back:

1. Fear of failure — Fear of failure affects people in many endeavors and in this case it could provide a convenient excuse for avoiding or delaying using the Program.

2. Fear of success — This is a fear that may surprise you. But many people do fear change. More than that they fear the *consequences* of change. For example, an individual may be subconsciously anxious about avoiding social contacts and relationships with others. Avoiding using a Program like this, or failing to progress on it, provides a convenient way of avoiding becoming more attractive to others. And a self-image which tells you that you are not attractive provides a convenient excuse for avoiding those kinds of relationships.

3. Habit — Some people have simply formed the habit of not changing. They find themselves in a "comfortable rut" and they never really explore or try to experience new things.

4. Procrastination — Procrastination is generally an indication of some inner tension or anxiety. It also serves as a convenient way to avoid activities and relationships with others. This leads to more anxiety and more inner tension and so the natural result is that it's followed by more delaying and avoiding. The cycle is completed as these actions reinforce a poor self-concept and may even result in a sense of failure or hopelessness.

Any of these factors could cause you to delay using the Program, or even inhibit your progress on it, without your even being aware of the real cause of the problem. *But if you can identify the cause, and confront it, you'll be well on your way to overcoming it.*

HOW TO INSURE
YOUR SUCCESS ON THE PROGRAM

The fascinating thing about the *Bio-Imagery Programming* process is that it inherently provides a way to help overcome most of these obstacles. That's why it's so vitally important to use the Program consistently. The benefits of improving your self-image go far beyond the intrinsic benefits of improving your figure. And each section of the Script has been carefully designed to help you enhance your self-image. So make a firm decision right now to pursue your own personal Program enthusiastically. Let go of your old self-image. Design a new improved self-image that is uniquely your own. In the next chapter you'll find a special Script that's been designed to help you to reach your full potential — not only on the Program, but in many other aspects of your life as well. So keep pursuing your goal . . . it's a goal that's well worth working for. And *believe* that you can reach it. You'll soon find yourself on the way to a lovelier more attractive figure . . . and, more importantly, a self-image that lets you say "You know, I really *do* like myself".

THE SELF-IMAGE SCRIPT

Since the self-image plays such a vital role in expediting the learning process, it's helpful to enhance the self-image in every way possible. In this chapter we discussed many helpful techniques that you can use to overcome procrastination, plateaus, and slow starts on the Program. In chapter 14 you will find another useful tool: the Self-Image Script.

The Self-Image Script is an independent program that

can provide benefits with or without the use of the figure development Program. For enhancing your self-image, improving your effectiveness, or for just getting more out of your life, you can enjoy and benefit from this Script.

But you may also find it helpful to use on occasion as you pursue your figure development objectives. Use it to enhance and reinforce the figure development Scripts by substituting this Script once or twice a week – or perhaps just as an "extra". You may find it helpful in removing some of the learning barriers that now and then surface from an oppositional self-image. This Script provides an ideal supplementary reinforcement procedure for the basic Program. It helps you to focus on body-image and not just on physical attributes.

The relaxation portion of the Script is quite similar to the relaxation portions of Scripts One and Two. However, for your convenience, it is included with the Script to enable you to proceed directly through the Script in proper sequence. But, since you've already learned a great deal about the art of relaxing, it is divided into three parts. Start with Part 1 when you wish to follow the complete relaxation portion of the Program. Start with parts 2 or 3 if you feel you are a "pro" at relaxing quickly, and you wish to get to the *Bio-Images* in as short a time as possible.

Here are several different ways in which the Self-Image Script can be used:

1. Use it to enhance the effectiveness of your figure development Program.
   A. Substitute the Self-Image Script once or twice weekly for either the Basic or Accelerated Scripts; or,
   B. Use it as an extra once or twice weekly. (If you are learning to relax very quickly you may occasionally omit Parts 1 and 2 of this Script

and begin with Part 3.)

2. Use it as an independent Program to help you enhance your self-image and improve your effectiveness at achieving *other* goals in your life. You'll find that this Script can be beneficial to you long after you have reached your figure development goals. To help you enhance your self-image, improve your efficiency and effectiveness, this Script, used independently, can provide life-long benefits.

3. Use Parts 1 and 2 of the Script separately for general relaxation and stress release. This section of the Script stands on its own as a useful and effective relaxation Program. You'll find that setting aside a few minutes daily for sheer relaxation can be highly beneficial to you.

4. Use Parts 1 and 2 as an "open-ended" introduction to personal "goal-setting visualizations" which you create in your own mind. The achievement of any goal begins with a strong visual image which you create in your own mind. Using Progressive Relaxation as a prelude to these visualizations can help you to reach your goals more easily.

Using the Script in this way is easy. Simply go through Parts 1 and 2 of the Script. Then, instead of proceeding through the balance of the Script, *create in your own mind mental pictures of the personal goals that you wish to achieve.* These visualizations, created while you are in a relaxed frame of mind, can be an important factor in helping you to achieve the goals you have set for yourself.

CHAPTER THIRTEEN
CHAPTER REFERENCES

The detailed publishing information for each of the following chapter references can be found in the bibliography in the Reading and Study Guide at the back of the book. For easy reference the appropriate section of the bibliography is shown in roman numerals following each of the references listed below.

1. Packard, J., 1981 (IV)
2. LeCron, L.M., 1969 (IV)
3. Williams, J.E., 1974 (IV)

14

The Maximum Effects Program

BREAKTHROUGH™
BIO-IMAGERY PROGRAMMING™

THE SELF-IMAGE SCRIPT
A Maximum Effect Program

PART ONE

This program to assist you in improving your self-image and your effectiveness is a simple and effective method. You will find it easy and enjoyable. Just let yourself relax and follow the simple procedures.

First, make yourself as comfortable as you can by sitting back in a soft easy chair or by lying comfortably on your back in your bed or on a couch. Take a moment to loosen any tight clothing. Take off your shoes so that you will be more comfortable and relaxed. Place your arms alongside your body in a *comfortable* and relaxed position or fold them over your body, whichever is more comfortable, and *begin* to relax the muscles of your whole body. Now as you begin to relax, *think* carefully about the instructions you are reading or hearing*.

While you are relaxing, simply follow the instructions and suggestions that you read or hear (or think about from memory). You will find it easy to follow these *suggestions* and *instructions.*

As you learn to follow these suggestions you will find that you become even more comfortable and have an enjoyable experience. The Program is easy and is quite natural. It requires no special effort. Just relax and let it happen and the Program will work automatically. Remember, you can be sure the Program works so you can be confident. You will find it is easy if you just *let it happen almost by itself.* The key words are: let yourself feel comfortable; let yourself relax and enjoy it; you will find it *pleasant and easy.*

The next few minutes is a time to learn to relax totally. It is a time to let the stresses of the day fade away and let the daily tensions drain away. *Your Program* will

*RECORDED VERSIONS OF THE SELF-IMAGE SCRIPT:
The current popularity of Talking Books demonstrates that many people prefer the convenience of learning information from recordings. Using recordings helps many people to learn *faster* and assimilate the learning process more *completely.* Although a tape or record is not essential for learning the method, it can expedite the process of learning this information just as it can any other information presented this way. No medical claims are made for the recordings. For those who prefer this convenience, these Scripts are available in professionally recorded form in a choice of either 12" LP record or cassette. For information write to: New Directions, Inc., Suite 208, Dept. BK-200, 161 Ottawa, N.W., Grand Rapids, Michigan 49503.

help you to feel more refreshed and feel more effective — even more alive and vibrant. *As you relax,* you will learn automatically to feel more and more comfortable. You will find that each time you listen to or read this Program and relax, it becomes easier and easier.

You are already learning to relax and feel more comfortable. You have already learned the first lesson without effort as you learn to relax. In time you will learn to relax quickly and effectively with or without the Script.

Now, as you lie or sit comfortably, you will begin to find that you breathe more easily and effortlessly. You can learn to relax easily as you say to yourself the words, *"I can relax now and breathe comfortably. This is my time to relax."* Just *thinking* these words helps you to relax. You are learning to use these words as your own personal Program. You can even reduce these words to simply "relax now" to let you drain away the tensions of your body, and enjoy deeper and deeper relaxation. Listening to the recording or reading this script, or just mentally thinking about the ideas presented here, helps this process of relaxing and enjoying. So say to yourself, as you do: "Just RELAX NOW: RELAX NOW; RELAX NOW." See how it becomes easier and easier and more and more pleasant.

Now you are learning to relax and feel comfortable. Good. Let the strain and tensions in your body drain away, slip away. You feel more comfortable.

Now as you are learning to relax and have pleasant feelings you can enjoy relaxation even more. Just take a long, comfortable breath and exhale slowly, and comfortably. *(PAUSE) Now do this again and feel the tension draining away.* (PAUSE) Now *visualize or see in your mind's eye,* a peaceful, relaxing picture of yourself as you feel yourself *drifting* into a deeper state of relaxation. Now take one more breath, slowly and comfortably. *Feel* yourself drifting, carefree; *see* yourself drifting, floating, more and more relaxed. Enjoy this feeling. Just drift — comfortable, relaxed, and *carefree.*

PART 2

Begin now to relax *all* the muscles of your body letting them become as loose and as limp as possible. Let's work with one leg first. Choose either leg and tighten the muscles of that leg — making the leg *feel* tight and rigid all over. Keep your leg muscles tight for a while. (PAUSE) Now let your leg muscles begin to relax from your toes up to your hip. Focus your attention first on your toes, letting them relax . . . then focus on the muscles in your lower leg, letting them relax . . . then focus on the muscles in your thigh, letting them relax. That's good. Now tighten up all the muscles of your leg again, and hold them tight for a while . . . then let them relax just as before, starting with your toes and going up the leg until your whole leg is quite relaxed. As you relax the muscles of your leg, feel the tensions drain away. Enjoy this feeling as you rest comfortably for a moment. OK, that's fine.

Now, tighten up your stomach muscles; pull your stomach in tight, hold your stomach that way for a few moments. Feel how tight your stomach is. (PAUSE) Now let your stomach muscles relax. As your stomach muscles relax, you relax, you feel comfortable and more relaxed. See how good this feels!

Now do the same thing with your chest and breathing muscles — by breathing in and holding your chest tight. Tighten the chest muscles first. Then let them relax and let the air out of your lungs. (PAUSE) Do this again, and *feel* the relaxation.

Now focus on your shoulders and your shoulder

muscles. Tighten them by pulling your shoulders back; *feel* how tight they are. Now, let the muscles of your shoulders relax. *Feel* the relaxation in your back.

Now stretch your neck by pushing your head up and tighten your neck muscles. Again, hold your head this way for a moment. Now relax your neck muscles. See how good this feels.

Now do the same thing with the muscles in your arms from the shoulders right down to your fingertips. First, tighten these muscles, stretching your arms and fingers and tightening your muscles making them rigid; hold your muscles in your arms tight, even tighter for a while. Now, let your muscles from your shoulders right down to your fingertips relax. Do this again and see, once more, how relaxing this can be.

Now, tighten up your whole face. Tighten the muscles of your mouth, your chin, your cheeks, and your forehead. Hold your face that way for a few moments. Tight. Tighter. Now relax all the muscles of your face and feel the tensions in your face drain away. Feel the comfort in your face. Now do this again. First tightening your facial muscles, then holding them for a few moments, then letting your whole face relax. Now you can feel even more relaxed all over.

PART 3

Your whole body is relaxing. Relaxation is so pleasant and comfortable. Let go completely and enjoy it. As you relax your whole body, all tension seems to drain away and you find a new sense of comfort and well-being. Even your breathing is more relaxed. You begin to feel relaxed all over, and more and more comfortable. Your whole body is relaxed, and your mind is at ease and clear and you feel comfortable.

Now you can attain *even greater* relaxation of your body and your mind. You can use your mind to help you. It's so easy. Just imagine that you are standing at the top of a very pleasant stairway with nice colors and soft carpeting. This will become your 10-step stairway to even more comfort and relaxation. Now, *in your imagination* see yourself walking down this stairway, slowly, step-by-step, and as you walk take each step in time with the count. And as we count, see yourself stepping down with each count, step-by-step, walking down to greater comfort and more relaxation.

Step #1, relax. You begin to feel so relaxed and drowsy.

Now step down, #2, and feel more drowsy and relaxed, more comfortable.

Now #3, *getting more drowsy* and relaxed.

#4. Getting more and more comfortable and relaxed.

#5. You can feel the *soft carpeting* and feel more relaxed, more comfortable.

#6. Relaxed. Comfortable.

#7. More drowsy, more relaxed, more comfortable.

#8. Getting more relaxed, more comfortable.

#9. Relaxed. Comfortable.

#10. So drowsy, so comfortable, so relaxed. Your body and your mind are both relaxed.

Now continue to relax, more and more. You feel comfortable and relaxed. As you think effortlessly of every word, your mind and your body feel more and more relaxed. You are breathing in a more relaxed and comfortable manner. With each breath you take you find that you are becoming more relaxed, alert, and more comfortable.

You are learning to relax very comfortably. Just continue to relax, rest, and to read or listen.

Now that you have learned to relax, you have already

taken the first important step to enhancing your self-image and improving your effectiveness. Relaxation is the foundation for learning to enhance your self-image. It is *important to understand* that almost all people who fail to live up to their capacities do so because they are inwardly anxious and tense — even though they may try to hide this from themselves and from others by pretending that they are happy and carefree. As you relax, you can accept the fact that some things in your past life added to your insecurity and lack of self-confidence. A basic cause of this insecurity is your poor self-concept — your poor self-image. But, now that you understand that, you can change your self-concept. With the help of this Script, and in a relaxed frame of mind, you can become a *winner,* and gain *self-confidence* and find that you have less need — less compulsion to delay and avoid goal achieving activities. You will find that you can improve your effectiveness, enjoy life more, and gain self-confidence. You will find that you can enjoy being decisive, and active, and accomplishing your goals and gaining self-confidence.

As you continue to relax, ask yourself "Why have I lacked self-confidence?" "What has made me feel insecure in the past?" There are only a few basic reasons for this. You may have been fearful that you would not be liked, or would be criticized. Or, you may have been afraid that you would be a failure. You might be afraid of success and the independence it brings. Or, you may have been anxious about your relationships with other people. Such things lead to anxiety, to inner tension, and so to insecurity and lack of self-confidence. It can even lead to a sense of failure or hopelessness.

But, now you are changing all of that. As you relax, and the tension drains away, you can begin the process of *internalizing* a good, healthy self-image. Each time you follow this Program, you will automatically improve your self-concept, lose tension, and gain self-confidence. You will begin to see that you have a lot to offer, that you are worthwhile, that — as you accept yourself more and more — other people will also accept you more and more and like you more and more. You begin to *feel* that you are basically *good* and *desirable* and *capable*. And as you gain self-confidence, your inner tensions slip away, and you feel good about yourself — and you can live as you should live, enjoyably and effectively — without tension, and without guilt.

It is important to remember that, *like all other people,* you will sometimes make mistakes. But, like all other people, you are good, you are worthwhile, and you can profit from mistakes, and with increasing self-confidence feel more self-assured, feel more secure, and succeed in reaching your goal of being an effective, happy, attractive person — efficient, decisive, and goal achieving.

BIO-IMAGE #1

Now, as you internalize these thoughts in a relaxed comfortable manner, and as you keep on gaining *self-confidence* and *inner security,* you can begin to *visualize* how you will *look, feel,* and *act* in all social situations. We shall call this visualization *Bio-Image* #1. Imagine, in your mind, that you are in a social situation with a few people around you. *Picture this scene in your mind.* See it vividly, in every detail. You are listening to them as they talk. You listen in a relaxed manner, feeling secure, comfortable, and self-assured. Then, when you are ready, you say something to your friends in response to what they have been talking about. You say this easily, comfortably and with complete self-assurance. As you speak, you show how self-assured you are, how you like yourself, and how you know you are also liked. Your friends look at this *new you* with surprise and delight. They envy you. They admire you. And now you realize that you are likeable for what you are — for the *real you.* You literally *eat up* their admiration, their liking for you, and you *feel deeply* that you are likeable and have much to offer. Your inner security increases, your inner tensions dissolve, and you feel great! You have begun to *internalize* an improved self-image. Remember that each time you follow this Script you will *see* and *feel* this mental picture more and more vividly; you will see the new *you* emerging, the new self-confident, self-assured you: a likeable, attractive, self-assured person. *Bio-Image* #1 will help you to gain increasing self-confidence each time you visualize it and help you drain away unnecessary anxiety and guilt about yourself.

Now, as you continue to relax we will go on to some other mental pictures that will teach your body how to function more effectively.

BIO-IMAGE #2

Here is *Bio-Image #2.* Imagine now that you are looking at some photographs, and you come upon a picture of an extremely attractive person with ideal posture and figure. You now look at this picture more closely. Suddenly, you realize that this is the *real you.* You look at the picture even more closely. Yes, it is you. You see this *new you* very clearly. You see a very attractive person who looks and feels poised and self-assured. You look terrific! You study the picture in greater detail. You admire how energetic and happy you look. You become more and more excited as you look at this picture of you. You look great — in excellent physical condition — healthy and self-assured. You *feel* how attractive you are. You *feel* good physically all over. You notice how well-dressed you are and how happy, relaxed, and calm and worry-free you are. Your eyes seem sparkling and smiling. You are smiling pleasantly. You *feel* vibrant, glowing with health and energy. As you continue to look at this mental picture, you can *feel* yourself becoming more attractive — and getting more and more like the picture. You feel proud of yourself.

Now you can picture yourself as you will be by the end of this Program — confident, self-assured, and effective — just like the photograph. In your mind visualize yourself as you stand in front of a full length mirror. See how attractive you look and feel. See how great you look. See yourself vividly, clearly — with your beautifully improved, self-confident manner. You have now enhanced the process of self-image improvement. You have begun to see how you can really look and feel.

Now you can relax even more and your body and your mind feel comfortable, and pleasantly, deeply relaxed.

BIO-IMAGE #3

And now we can turn to *Bio-Image #3*.

You are relaxing even more fully now. As you relax picture in your mind a giant movie screen. As you watch, the movie begins, and you see that the same slender, attractive you that you saw in the photograph is the star. You are the star and the director of this film.

As the scene opens the camera focuses on you as you begin your day. You expect another great day. You are smiling and feel a deep down sense of joy and exhilaration as you look forward to an enjoyable day. You feel a sense of optimism and enthusiasm and positive expectancy as you start another great day. You see and feel how great you look — how energetic and healthy and happy you look — and how easily and smoothly and gracefully you move with your trim, well-proportioned, attractive body.

You are now living the part of the role. It is you, and you see and feel yourself in every scene.

The major scenes in the movie show you enjoying a full and rich, happy life filled with interesting and exciting things to do. As you go through the day you notice how calm and worry-free you are. You notice how things don't seem to bother or upset you. You handle your life with secure, mature confidence. You see yourself having fun — enjoying your life and life's activities. Your life is occupied with interesting and exciting things to do. You see yourself enjoying your work and your many social activities, personal relationships, and hobbies. Your work activities are efficient and effective. You are meeting new people and forming new friendships. As you meet other people they are impressed with how friendly and nice you are. As you become a part of the movie you actually feel, as you live and experience the part, the positive emotions that are part of your improved self-image. You feel a reassuring sense of self-confidence. You feel assured and secure. You feel pride in your life and your life's activities. And you feel a sense of optimism and enthusiasm.

You feel that this is the *real you* now controlling your own life and your own activities. You know and feel how worthwhile you are and how much you *deserve* to succeed, to be happy, and to achieve your goals.

You see yourself as you do things promptly. You see and feel how decisive you are — reaching decisions promptly and wisely and then acting on them right away.

And as you feel the positive, happy feelings, you feel the negative feelings you used to have disappearing — like being erased from a blackboard. You feel leaving you the fears of failure, fears of criticism, fears of success and independence, fears of decisions — all the fears that you used to have. You feel leaving you negative procrastinating habits, fears of social and personal relationships and committments. You feel these and other negative and other self-defeating notions leaving you. You watch as they disappear from the blackboard and you feel a sense of elation and joy and exhilaration and freedom as they leave you.

You watch as they disappear just as if they were in helium filled balloons floating away out of sight in the sky. They leave to make room for a new life of freedom for the real you, the new you. Their place is filled with positive self-expectancy, enthusiasm, optimism, joy and happiness, and positive self-esteem and self-confidence.

You feel great as feelings of joy, happiness, excitement, energy, and creativity dominate your mind. You feel good about yourself and know how you desire to succeed and how you deserve to succeed. You feel a sense of freedom at being able to control and direct your life. You enjoy your new independence and feel a sense of pride in the new you, the real you.

BIO-IMAGE #4

And now a fourth *Bio-Imagery* picture will assist you even more in enjoying a sense of self-confidence, happiness, and effectiveness.

See yourself in your own mind looking the way you've always dreamed of, and feeling tremendously proud of yourself and your life. You feel confident and proud of the way you look. People admire your appearance and they admire you. You have no guilt about being attractive — only confidence and mature pride. With an attractive appearance you feel proud and confident. You like yourself, and others like you. You feel secure and self-assured. You are very pleased with yourself and the way you look. Everything seems right. You look radiantly happy, confident, and proud. You feel pleased that others are friendly to you and admire you.

You are delighted at how well you feel as you move so gracefully and easily. You feel great about your new self-confidence. And every day you feel better and better about yourself.

As you visualize *Bio-Image* #4 you are in a very deep state of total relaxation. Very comfortable. Very relaxed. And your mind focuses on, and remembers the four *Bio-Images*. Twice daily you will enjoy relaxing for a short period of time and vividly picture the four *Bio-Images*.

Bio-Image #1 — Visualize the self-confidence and inner security that you feel and show in all social situations. Feel how self-assured, likeable, and attractive you have become.

Bio-Image #2 — See a photograph of how attractive and self-assured you look. See how terrific you look at the end of this Program.

Bio-Image #3 — See a movie of the new you enjoying your life and your life's activities.

Bio-Image #4 — Enjoy a feeling of great pride about your confident and attractive appearance.

Twice each day, you will enjoy relaxing and setting aside a brief period of time to visualize these *Bio-Images.* And you will enjoy following this Script on a regular basis.

Each time that you read or listen to this Script you will enter a deeper, more comfortable stage of relaxation. Each time you read or listen you will find that you relax more quickly. And each time that you say to yourself the words "RELAX NOW" you will be able to relax completely, immediately, and will then visualize the 4 *Bio-Images.* This Script, and the 4 *Bio-Images,* used consistently, will assure you of achieving your self-improvement goals. You will become more attractive and you will look and feel great. Following this Program on a regular basis will help you to relax, relieve stress and tension, and enable you to achieve your self-improvement goals.

And now, to conclude this Script, count to 5 after which you will feel wide awake, happy, and refreshed.

1. Feeling good, feeling pleasant, getting up.
2. More alert, refreshed, enthusiastic.
3. Stretching your arms and legs and body — feeling good, refreshed.
4. Eyes wide open, feeling wonderful.
5. More alert, feeling refreshed, and vigorous.

PART VI

Your Resource Guide: Questions and Answers About The Program

15

Questions and Answers About The Method

From time to time as you are using this Program you may have questions about the method itself, the results it can achieve, or specific questions about its use. This chapter provides a summary of the most commonly asked questions about the Program.

Q. What is this new method?
A. It's a simple, effective way to increase breast size in the same natural way that the breasts first began to develop in early adolescence.

Q. How does it work?
A. It works by simply improving circulation in the breast area. Proper circulation is vital for the growth of any part of the body because it's the blood that brings the nutrients essential for

growth.

Q. How was it discovered?

A. Thousands of people have already learned how to improve circulation for a variety of purposes, and they use these simple methods every day. For more than a decade scientists have been showing people how easily they can use these proven methods at home. But, until recently, no one ever thought to see if improving circulation in the breast area would increase breast size in women of virtually any age (even years after the developmental stage had passed). Then, some independent teams of researchers and medical doctors, working separately in different parts of the country, conducted the clinical studies which signaled this exciting scientific breakthrough.

Q. What were the results of these studies?

A. All women participating in the studies achieved measurable increases in actual breast size (not just the size of the back or chest muscles). Average increases of total breast size in two independent clinical studies were approximately two inches with increases ranging as high as 3.54 inches.

Q. Does this method help reduce sagging?

A. Yes, in most cases. The medical doctor who conducted one of the studies stated that all of the women in the study reported that they were very pleased with the resulting firmness and fullness of the breasts.

Q. Are there other benefits from this technique that

were reported in the studies?

A. Several. For example, the doctor stated that the women in the study who previously had breasts of uneven size reported that their breasts were even in size by the conclusion of the study[1]. In another study women reported the reduction of bulgy waistlines in addition to the increase in breast size. Other studies on breast enlargement indicate that positive changes can occur in many other aspects of life including improved self-esteem and self-confidence, as well as improved interpersonal and marital relationships.

Q. Is the technique difficult to learn?

A. It's amazingly simple! It can be learned in the privacy of your own home in just a few minutes a day.

Q. Is it safe?

A. Totally. It is not an artificial Program. It's designed to help you to reinstate the *natural* increases in breast size that began in your early adolescence.

Q. Does it involve physical exercise?

A. No. The fact is that exercise cannot help you increase the actual size of your breasts for a very simple reason — the breasts contain no muscles. This new method requires no physical effort of any kind — in fact you use it while you are resting.

Q. Does it use any of the protein or enzyme supplements I've seen advertised?

A. No. These products are designed to help you gain weight on the assumption that some of that weight will be in your breasts. Unfortunately, much of the excess weight will have to go to other parts of the body as well.

Q. Why don't more people know about the clinical studies for this new method?

A. Knowledge is currently growing at a phenomenal rate. It's just impossible for scientists, doctors, and the public to know about all the new developments unfolding in every field of knowledge. It often takes five to ten years for new discoveries to become widely-known.

Q. Obviously, this new method does not involve surgery.

A. That is correct. Prior to the publication in scientific journals of the results of the clinical studies for this new method, surgery was the only other breast enlargement procedure with clinical evidence for its effectiveness. Other methods, some very heavily advertised, have been unable to cite actual studies on which their procedures or products are based.

Q. Are there disadvantages to surgery?

A. Yes. In addition to the expense of the procedure, there are the disadvantages of possible scarring, the possibility of unnatural looking results, the discomfort, and the dangers from the anesthetics and possible infections. Complication rates as high as 60 percent have been reported for breast enlargement surgery[2].

Q. What are the advantages of the new method?

A. It's safe. It's easy-to-use. It's economical. It's

natural. And it can be used in the privacy of your own home in just a few minutes a day by women of virtually any age. Best of all it really works.

Q. How long does it take each day?
A. Just a few minutes a day while you're learning the method. After it's learned it can take as little as 1 or 2 minutes a day.

Q. How long does it take to begin to see results?
A. Typically within 2 to 3 weeks. (Occasionally, some cases show results a little later.) Then, the increases can continue for up to 12 weeks or more.

Q. When will I have my greatest progress?
A. Although individuals vary, most women seem to enjoy their greatest increases in the second month of the Program.

Q. Is any special time of the day preferable for using the Program?
A. The best time is simply the time that's most convenient for you. However, a set time each day has the advantage of helping you form the habit of sticking to the Program.

Q. What if I miss a day?
A. Just get back on the Program the next day. The Program has adequate leeway built in for occasional variations. But if a lovelier figure is really important to you, keep after your goal.

Q. I would like to reach my goal in less than 12 weeks. Is this possible?

A. Some people do. But it's important to be realistic. The original growth of your breasts during adolescence took much longer than 12 weeks. Since you really want to reach your goal, persist in your endeavors and follow the full Program.

Q. Is age a factor?
A. Apparently not, at least within the wide age limits that have been studied. In one of the studies the ages of the women ranged as high as 54 years.

Q. How much can be gained?
A. In the studies scientists verified gains up to 3.54 inches. Actual users of the *New Dimensions* Program report gains up to 4½ inches ... and, occasionally, as high as 6 to 8 inches.

Q. What if I want further gains later, can I repeat the Program?
A. Yes. One of the researchers recommends that after you complete your Program that you wait for 3 months and then repeat the entire Program again. He reports that the gains continue in the second phase[3].

Q. I am planning a diet. Can I go on it and still use the Program?
A. Yes.

Q. I have tried other methods and they didn't work for me. Why is that?
A. Quite honestly, the only effective methods of breast enlargement, confirmed by scientific research, are this method and surgery.

Q. I wish to gain just a small increase. Can I limit the amount of increase?

A. Yes. Just use the Program until you have reached your goal and then discontinue it.

Q. My waist is already very small. Can I increase breast size without reducing my waistline?

A. Yes. The results indicate that waist reduction typically takes place only for those women who would benefit from a reduction.

Q. Once I reach my goal will my breasts remain at their new larger size?

A. Yes. Although the Program includes a simple reinforcement technique that you may wish to use on occasion, professionals using the method report that they have generally found this unnecessary (Packard[4] and Wilson[5]).

Q. I once tried an exercise device and my back and arms got larger. Will this happen with this Program?

A. No. Since there is no exercise involved in this Program you will not build up your muscles. Instead you will benefit from a proportioning effect which enlarges the breasts and reduces the area immediately below the breasts, and often the waistline as well.

Q. How many inches will I gain?

A. Each individual is unique and results vary from person to person. Review the sample Progress Charts of women who have used the Program in chapters 11 and 12 and the letters from women who have used the Program in chapter 1 to get an idea of the kind of results women have achieved.

Q. Can the Program be used while pregnant or nursing a child?

A. You'll enjoy a natural increase in breast size while you're pregnant so we recommend that you wait until after. You should ask your doctor if you have any questions regarding the use of the Program during these times.

Q. What if I get off to a slow start?

A. Give it a fair try. Many women who enjoyed excellent results with the Program were slow starters (see chapters 11-14).

Q. If I fall asleep while I am using the method will it still be effective?

A. It is most effective when you are totally relaxed but *alert*. It you try to read the Script, rehearse it in your mind, or listen to it when you are overly-tired you may become so relaxed that you fall asleep. If you find that you do, you can form the habit of remaining alert, although totally relaxed by (1) using the Program when you are reasonably refreshed, (2) sitting instead of lying down (keep your head up instead of leaning it back), and (3) setting one or more timers or buzzers next to you and have them go off at the approximate time you have been dozing off. You'll find that you will quickly *learn* to become totally relaxed while you continue thinking about the thoughts and images presented in the Scripts.

Q. I feel I have really mastered the relaxation portion of the Scripts and have learned to relax totally. Can I now shorten the relaxation section of the Script?

A. *After you have begun to achieve positive results* on the Program you may shorten the relaxation section of the Program as follows: use the full Script one day; then, the next day start your Program just prior to the section on muscle relaxation; then, the third day start it just prior to the 10-step relaxation segment (the approximate segment is close enough — it is not necessary to be exact). You may continue to alternate the starting point of the Script on this schedule as long as you feel that you are relaxing as effectively with the shorter relaxation time period — *and as long as you continue to get positive results from the Program.* For maximum benefit from the Program, however, you will find it helpful to use the complete Program periodically. This will help reinforce the learning process.

Q. Will exercise help?

A. Exercise is beneficial for many reasons — including your posture which, of course, affects the appearance of your breasts. It will not, however, increase actual breast size as this Program can.

Q. Are there reasons why my breasts did not grow as large as they could have when I was younger?

A. There could be many reasons. The developmental stages of a young girl's life are periods of hectic physical, bio-chemical, and emotional change. The demands on the body are at a peak. If you would like to explore this subject more fully, consult some of the references cited in the Reading and Study Guide.

Q. I've seen other similar programs advertised. Are they any good?

A. That depends totally on the expertise of the person developing the Program. You should be certain that any Program you use is designed by knowledgeable experts.

* * * * *

The questions and answers in this chapter are the result of extensive experience with the *New Dimensions* Program. Used in conjunction with the rest of the book, the essential information that you need to reach your goal is here for you to transpose into a realistic and enjoyable figure development Program.

Our journey, which began with an introduction to a new breast enlargement discovery, and took us on an interesting voyage through the scientific and practical aspects of the Program, now leads us to one inescapable conclusion: while the tour itself may be fascinating, it's the destination which is really far more important. It's the goal of a lovelier figure that, in the final analysis, is far more meaningful to you than all of the studies and all of the scientific data. The stories of the women who have used the Program provide eloquent testimony of the paramount importance of that goal. But the exciting thing is that now that goal can be transcribed into reality! Now a lovelier figure is within your reach. And every essential fact that you need to know to insure your success is here.

This book is your road map to that success. Follow it. Use it. Stick with it consistently. Make your journey to a lovelier figure a delightful and enjoyable experience. Success *is* within your reach.

CHAPTER FIFTEEN
CHAPTER REFERENCES

The detailed publishing information for each of the following chapter references can be found in the bibliography in the Reading and Study Guide at the back of the book. For easy reference the appropriate section of the bibliography is shown in roman numerals following each of the references listed below.

1. Willard, R.D., 1977 (IV)
2. Packard, J., 1981 (IV)
3. Williams, J.E., 1979 (IV)
4. Packard, J., 1981 (IV)
5. Wilson, D.L., 1979 (IV)

Research and
Study Guide

EXPLORING THE SCIENTIFIC DATA
FOR THE METHOD

The learning procedures integrated in the *Bio-Imagery Programming* process are based on, and enlarge upon, the results of actual studies conducted by scientific researchers and by medical doctors conducting separate clinical tests. For more than a decade scientific studies on learning procedures and related processes have demonstrated that individuals can alter bodily functions and processes formerly believed beyond human control. *Bio-Imagery Programming* is based on sound scientific data. For those interested in exploring the background for its development, and the extensive evidence for its scientific basis, the following information and the accompanying bibliography, provides more extensive information.

The entire program of relaxation and habit-training methods used in *Bio-Imagery Programming* is designed to encourage normal and natural development of the breasts and secondary improvement in self-assurance and self-respect. The procedures integrate the findings of psychological research and clinical practice, utilizing natural, psychological methods to improve circulatory processes as a means of improving breast development and enhancing the self-image.

The *Bio-Imagery Programming* process is based on the general and specific findings from the psychological fields of: learning theory; methods of inducing relaxation so as to induce more effective and harmonious general bodily processes; methods of insuring improvement in self-image and self-concept; psychological methods of learning feedback; methods of improved visualization and self-imagery; and the specific studies on the effects of some of these procedures, in both research studies under controlled conditions and in clinical studies under the supervision of qualified professionals. These studies demonstrate the effectiveness of these methods in improving general physiological functioning and specific and improved circulatory processes which assist in normal development of the breasts which may have been inhibited by such factors as: undue tension; inability to focus on one's own natural bodily processes; inability to maintain relaxed concentration; and inhibition in normal learning processes.

Listed in the attached bibliography are the studies demonstrating these effects and, in particular, the studies which demonstrate the specific effects on breast development.

The massive body of knowledge accumulated in these areas over the past three decades, in particular, and the applied techniques utilized in the *Bio-Imagery Programming* method, are effectively utilized in this carefully designed learning procedure.

In addition to the knowledge from thousands of

psychological studies, *Bio-Imagery Programming* integrates the knowledge and the techniques derived from research and psychological, clinical studies pertaining directly to improvement in growth processes affecting the breasts. Samplings of these studies are included in the bibliography which follows. It should be noted, especially, that none of these methods employs medical devices or techniques, none utilizes the ingestion of any product, and none offers any medical advice or suggestion. Instead, the methods are based on learning processes — they are strictly psychological and are presented so as to encourage more effective and more natural bodily processes through time and research-tested psychological principles and methods.

The more general psychological studies on which *Bio-Imagery* is based, as well as the more specific and directly-related psychological studies, are noted in the bibliography.

The approach and methods used in *Bio-imagery Programming* are based on hundreds of studies and experiments, some of them specifically directed to investigating the possibilities for improving body-figure and to gaining enlargement of the breasts.

Over the years it has been learned that people can change not only their behavior and personality, but also their physiological processes, bodily functions, and bodily structure to gain better self-concepts and more effective body-functions. Such methods were used in ancient times, but their more recent use is based on learning studies, studies in psychology, and especially studies on developmental and learning processes. Many theories have been developed to explain the findings from these studies, but no one theory can do justice to all of the findings.

Bio-Imagery Programming is based on these scientific findings and integrates them into a manageable, practical form, so that thousands more can take advantage of the new knowledge. We cannot attempt to provide a comprehensive listing of all of the relevant studies and books based on these studies, but will offer a selected list of relevant references. As will be seen, these references include: I *Learning Theory and Methods,* II *Relaxation Methods and Visual Imagery,* III *Psychological Methods of Therapeutic Change* (including conditioning methods), and, IV *Research and Reports on Psychological Factors in Normal Breast Growth.* The references cited under this last heading are immediately relevant to the methods described in this book. Several of the scientific studies cited have demonstrated the significant and remarkable results which can be achieved using these psychological procedures. The relevant independent clinical studies were conducted by research scientists and reported in highly respected scientific journals found in most major universities. All of the tests were carefully documented and used appropriate scientific procedures. In addition to those specific clinical studies documenting the relevant research on this newly explored breast enlargement method, this listing (section IV) includes related references on research and reports on psychological factors in normal breast growth.

You will find that some of the references cited in our bibliography are highly technical while others do not require scientific sophistication. Browse through this list and, if interested, select and read those which are relevant for you.

SUGGESTED READINGS
AND BIBLIOGRAPHY

I. Learning Theory and Methods

Allport, G.W., & Vernon, P.E. Studies in Expressive Movement, N.Y.: Macmillan, 1933.

Allyn, J., & Festinger, L. The effectiveness of unanticipated persuasive communication. *J. Abn. Soc. Psychol.*, 1961, *62*, 35-40

Anasti, A., & Foley, J.P. *Differential Psychology*, 3rd ed. N.Y.: Macmillan 1958.

Beeby, C.E. An experimental investigation into the simultaneous constituent acts of skill. *Brit. J. Psychol.*, 1930, *20*, 336-353.

Block, J. Studies in the phenomenology of emotion. *J. Abn. Soc. Psychol.*, 1957, *54*, 358-363.

Berger, L., & McGaugh, J.L. Critique and reformulation of learning theory: approaches to psychotherapy and neurosis. *Psychol. Bull.*, 1965, *63*, 338-358.

Brown, J.S. Gradients of approach and avoidance responses and their relation to motivation. *J. Compar. Physiol. Psychol.*, 1948, *41*, 450-465.

Bruner, J., & Kennedy, D. Habituation: Occurrence at a neuromuscular junction. *Science*, 1970, *169*, 92-94.

Christensen, B.N., & Martin, A.R. Estimates of probability transmiier release at the mammalian neuromuscular junction. *J. Physiol. Psychol.*, 1970, *210*, 933-945.

Estes, W.K. Learning theory and the new "mental chemistry". *Psychol. Rev.*, 1960, *67*, 207-223.

Field, J.H., et al (Eds.) *Handbook of Physiology, Section I. Neurophysiology.* Baltimore: Waverly, 1959.

Funkenstein, D.H., et al. *Mastery of Stress.* Cambridge, Mass.: Harvard Univ. Press, 1957.

Gardner-Medwin, A.R. Modifiable synapses necessary for learning. *Nature*, 1969, *223*, 916-919.

Hebb, D.O. *The Organization of Behavior*, N.Y.: Wiley, 1946.

Hebb, D.O. Concerning Imagery. *Psychol. Rev.*, 1968, *75*, 466-477.

Hilgard, E.R., & Bower, G. *Theories of Learning*, 3rd ed. N.Y.:

Appleton, 1966.

Hilgard, E.R. *Divided Consciousness: Multiple Controls in Human Thought and Action,* N.Y.: John Wiley & Sons, 1977.

Hilgard, E.R., & Marquis, D.R. *Conditioning and Learning,* 2nd ed. N.Y. Appleton, 1961

Jouvet, M. The state of sleep. *Sci. Amer.,* 1967, *216,* 62-72.

Kimmel, H.D. Habituation, habituability and conditioning. *Behavorial Studies,* ed. Peeke & Hertz, 1973, 219-238. N.Y. Academic Press, 1973.

Kornblith, C., & Olds, J. Unit activity in brain stem reticular formation of the rat during learning. *J. Neurophysiol.,* 1973, *36,* 489-501.

Kranse, F.B., & Bryan, J.S. Habituation: Regulation through presynaptic inhibition, *Science,* 1973, *182,* 590-592.

Kretch, D., et al. *Elements of Psychology,* 2nd ed. N.Y.: Knopf, 1969.

Leuba, C., & Dunlap, R. Conditioning imagery. *J. Exper. Psychol.,* 1951, *41,* 252-355.

Leuba, C., & Boteman, D. Learning During Sleep. *American Journal of Psychol.,* 1952, *65,* 301-302.

Lukowiak, K., & Jacklet, J.W. Habituation and dishabituation. *Science,* 1972, *178,* 1306-1308.

Marquis, D.P. Can Conditioned responses be established in the newborn infant? *J. Genet. Psychol.,* 1931, *39,* 479-492.

Miller, L.A. Conunctive concept learning as affected by prior relevance information and other informational variables. *J. Exp. Psychol.,* 1974, *103,* 1220-1223.

Miller, N.E. Interaction Between Learned and Physical Factors in Mental Illness. In C.M. Franks & Wilson, G.T. *Annual Review of Behavior Therapy: Theory and Practice.* N.Y.: Bruner-Mazel.

Miller, N.E. Learning of Visceral and Glandular Responses. *Science,* 1967, *163,* 434-445.

Norman, N.F. Effects of overlearning, problem shifts, and probablisitic reinforcement in discrimination learning. In Krantz, D.H., et al. (Eds.) *Contemporary Developments in Mathematical Psychology Vol. I: Learning, Memory and Thinking.* San Francisco: Freeman, 1974.

Papez, J.W. A proposed mechanism of emotion. *Arch. Neurol. Psychiat. Chicago*. 1937, *38*, 725-743.

Pavlov, I.P. *Conditioned Reflexes*. London: Oxford, 1927.

Restle, F. The selection of strategies in cue learning. *Psychol. Rev.* 1962, *69*, 329-343.

Richardson, A. *Mental Imagery*, N.Y. Springer, 1969.

Rock, I. The role of repetition in associative learning. *Amer. J. Psychol.*, 1957, *70*, 186-193.

Rundus, D. Negative effects of using list items as recall cues. *J. Learn. Verbal Behav.*, 1973, *12*, 43-50.

Scandura, J.M. *Structural Learning: Theory and Research*. N.Y.: Gordon & Breach, 1973.

Schafer, R., & Murphy, G. The role of autism in figure-ground relationship. *J. Exper. Psychol.*, 1943, *32*, 335-343.

Seamon, J.G. Retrieval processes for long-term storage. *J. Exper. Psychol.*, 1973, *98*, 170-176.

Shapiro, D., Tursky, B., & Schwartz, G.E. Differentiation of heart rate and Systabolic Blood Pressure in Man by Operant Conditioning. *Psychosomatic Medicine*, 1970, *32*, 417-423.

Simon, C. & Emmons, W. Learning During Sleep. *Psychol. Bull.*, 1955, *52*, 328-342.

Skinner, R.B. *Science and Human Behavior*, N.Y.: Macmillan, 1953.

Sperry, R.W. Cerebral organization and Behavior. *Science*, 1961, *133*, 1749-1753.

Stampil, T. The Effects of Frequency or Repetition on the Retention of Auditory Material Presented During Sleep. Masters Thesis, Loyola U. 1953.

Teitelbaum, T. Motivational correlates of hypothalamic activity. *Excerpts. Medica. Int. Congr. Series*, 1962, *47*, 697-704.

Theios, J., et al. Memory scanning as a serial self-terminating process. *J. Exper. Psychol.*, 1973, *97*, 322-336.

Tolman, E.C. *Purposive Behavior in Animals*, N.Y.: Appleton, 1967.

Trabasso, L., & Bower, G.H. *Attention in Learning: Theory and Research*. N.Y.: Wiley, 1968.

White, R.W. Motivation reconsidered: The concept of competence. *Psychol. Rev.*, 1959, *66*, 297-333.

Young, P.T. *Motivation and Emotion*. N.Y.: Wiley, 1961.

II. Relaxation Methods and Visual Imagery

Arnheim, R. *Visual Thinking*. Barkeley, Calif.: Univ. of Calif. Press, 1972

Barber, T.X., et al. (Eds.) *Biofeedback and Self-Control*. Chicago: Aldine Publ. Co., 1976.

Barber, T.X. Implications for human capabilities and potentialities: control of skin temperature. Biofeedback and Self-Control, 1975, 5, 58-60.

Barber, T.X. Suggested ("hypnotic") Behavior. Trance Paradigm versus an alternate Paradigm. In Fromm, E., & Shor, R.E. (Eds.) *Hypnosis Research Developments and Perspectives*. Chicago: Aldine-Atherton, 1972.

Barber, T.X. Physiological Effects of Hypnosis and Suggestion. Chicago: Aldine-Atherton, 1971.

Benson. H. *The Mind/Body Effect*. N.Y.: Simon and Schuster, 1979.

Benson, H. *The Relaxation Response*. N.Y.: William Morrow & Co. 1975.

Bergman, J.S. & Johnson, H.J. Sources of Information which affect Training and Raising of Heart Rate. Psychophysiology, 1972, 9, 30-39.

Bertini, M. Lewis, H.B. & Witkin, H.P. Some Preliminary Observations with an Experimental Procedure for the Study of Hypnotic States and Related Phenomenon. In Tart, CT. (Ed.) *Altered States of Consciousness* N.Y.: John Wiley & Sons, 1969.

Brown, B.B. *New Mind, New Body*, N.Y.: Harper & Row, 1974

Bry, A. *Visualization*. N.Y.: Harper & Row, 1978

Budzynski, T.H. Some applications of biofeedback produced twilight states. *Biofeedback and Self-Control*, 1973, 145-153.

Carson, J. Learning Without Pain. "Doctors Explain Suggestology" Toronto Globe, Mar. 9, 1971.

Delgado, J.M.R. *Physical Control of the Mind*. N.Y.: Harper & Row, 1969.

DeToledo, L., & Black, A.H. Heart rate: changes during conditioned suppression in rats. *Science*, 1966, 152, 1404-1406.

DiCara, L.V., et al. (Eds.) Biofeedback and Self-Control. Chicago: Aldine, 1975.

DiCara, L.V., and Miller, N.E. Instrumental learning of vasomoter responses in rats: Learning to respond differentially in the two ears. *Science,* 1968, *159,* 1485-1486.

Franks, C.M. *Behavior Therapy.* N.Y.: McGraw-Hill, 1969.

Franks, C.M., & Wilson, G.T. *Behavior Therapy: Theory and Practice.*

Gottschalk, L.A. Self-induced visual imagery, affect, arousal, and autonomic correlates. *Psychosomatics,* 1974, *4,* 1966.

Graham, C. & Liebowitz, H.W. The Effect of Ingestion on Visual Acuity. *International Journal of Clinical and Experimental Hypnosis,* 1972, *20,* 1969-186.

Green, A. & E. *Beyond Biofeedback.* N.Y.: Delacorte Press, 1977.

Green, E. Biofeedback for Mind-Body Self-Regulation: Healing and Creativity. Interdisciplinary Symposium, 10-30-71 (copyright 1972, Acadamy of Parapsychology and Medicine).

Hartmann, E. (Ed.) *Sleep and Dreaming.* Boston: Little, Brown & Co., 1970.

Hilgard, E.R. *Divided Consciousness. Multiple Controls in Human Thought and Action.* N.Y.: Wiley & Sons, 1977.

Isaacson, R.L. (Ed.) *Basic Readings in Neuropsychology.* N.Y.: Harper & Row, 1964.

Jacobsen, E. Neuromuscular controls in man: Methods of self-direction in health and disease. *Amer. J. Psychol.,* 1955, *68,* 549-561.

Jacobson, E. *Progressive Relaxation.* Chicago: Univ. of Chicago Press, 1938.

Kamia, J. Operant control of the EEG alpha rhythm and some of its reported effects on consciousness. In Tart, C.T. (Ed.) *Altered States of Consciousness.* N.Y.: Wiley, 1969.

Kanfer, F.H., & Phillips, J.S. *Learning Foundations of Behavior Therapy.* N.Y.: Wiley, 1970.

Karlins, M., & Andrews, L.M. *Biofeedback: Turning on the Power of Your Mind.* Phila: J.B. Lippincott Co., 1972.

Klinger, E. *Structure and Function of Fantasy.* N.Y.: Wiley & Sons, 1971.

Lacey, J.I. Individual differences in somatic response patterns. *J. Compar. Physiol. Psychol.,* 1950, *113,* 338-350.

Lazarus, A.A. Clinical Behavior Therapy. N.Y.: Brumer/Mazel, 1972.

Lazarus, R.S., J.C. Speisman, A.M. Modkoff, and L.A. Davidson. "A Laboratory Study of Psychological Stress produced by a Motion Picture Film." *Psychological Monographs,* 1962, *76.*

Leitenberg, H., et al. Feedback in behavioral modification. *J. Appl. Behavioral Analysis,* 1968, *1,* 131-137.

Leitenberg, H. (Ed.). Handbook of Behavior Modification and Behavior Therapy. Englewood-Cliff, New Jersey: Prentice-Hall, 1976.

Maltz, M., *Psychocybernetics,* N.Y.: Simon & Schuster, 1960

Marks, D.F. Individual differences in the vividness of imagery and their effects of function. In Sheehan, P. (Ed.) The Functions and Nature of Imagery. N.Y.: Academic Press, 1972.

Miller, N.E. Learning of visceral and glandular responses. *Science,* 1969, *163,* 434-445.

Miller, N.E. Learning glandular and visceral control of responses. *Current Status of Physiological Psychology,* 1972.

Ostrander, S. & Schroeder, L. *Super-Learning.* N.Y.: Delacorte Press, 1979.

Pelletier, K.R. *Mind as Healer Mind as Slayer.* N.Y.: Delacorte Press, 1977.

Roberts, A.H., et al. Individual differences in autonomic control. *J. Abn. Psychol.,* 1976, *84,* 272-279.

Segal, S.J. The Adaptive Functions of Imagery. N.Y.: Academic Press, 1971.

Selye, H. *The Stress of Life.* N.Y.: McGraw-Hill, 1956.

Selye, H. *Stress Without Distress.* Phila. & N.Y.: J.P. Lippincott, 1976.

Schultz, J.H. & Luther, W. *Autogenic Training: A Psychophysiologic Approach to Psychotherapy.* N.Y.: Grune & Stratton, 1959.

Spielberger, C.D. *Anxiety and Behavior.* N.Y.: Academic Press, 1966.

Weiskrantz, L. (Ed.) Analysis of Behavior Change. N.Y.: Harper & Row, 1968.

III. Psychological Methods of Therapeutic Change

Alexander, F., et al. *Psychoanalytic Therapy: Principles and Application* N.Y.: Ronald Press, 1954.

Bandura, A. Vicarious processes: A case of no-trial learning. In Berkowitz, E. (Ed.). *Advances in Social Psychology*, Vol. 2, N.Y.: Rinehart & Winston, 1963.

Bergin, A.E., & Strupp, H.H. *Changing Frontiers in the Science of Psychotherapy.* Chicago: Aldine-Atherton, 1972.

Binder, V., Binder, A., and Rimland, B. *Modern Therapies.* Englewood Cliffs, New Jersey, 1976.

Brenner, C. *An Elementary Textbook f Psychoanalysis,* Rev. New York: International Universities Press, 1973.

Burton, A. *Modern Humanistic Psychotherapy.* San Francisco: Jossey-Bass, 1967.

Carkhuff, R.R., & Berenson, B.G. *Beyond Counseling and Psychotherapy.* N.Y.: Holt, Rinehart & Winston, 1967.

Colby, K.M. *A Primer for Psychotherapists.* N.Y.: Ronald Press, 1951.

Ellis, A. Reason and Emotion in Psychotherapy. N.Y.: Lyle Stuart, 1962.

Fix, A.J., and Haffke, E.A. *Basic Psychological Therapies: Comparative Effectiveness.* N.Y.: Human Sciences Press, 1976.

Ford, D.H., & Urban, H.B. *Systems of Psychotherapy.* N.Y.: Wiley & Sons, 1967.

Freud, S. *The Problem of Anxiety.* N.Y.: Psychoanalytic Quarterly Press, 1936.

Fromm-Reichmann, F. *Principles of Intensive Psychotherapy.* Chicago: Univ. of Chicago Press, 1950.

Gill, M.M., & Brenman, M. *Hypnosis and Related States.* N.Y.: International Universities Press, 1967.

Hartmann, E. (Ed.). *Sleep and Dreaming.* Boston: Little, Brown, 1970.

Hutt, M.L. *Psychosynthesis: Vital Therapy.* Oceanside, N.Y.: Dabor Science Publications, 1977.

Hutt, M.L., & Isaacson, R.L. *The Science of Interpersonal Behavior.* N.Y.: Harper & Row, 1966.

Research and Study Guide

Langs, J. *The Therapeutic Interaction:* A Synthesis. N.Y.: Jason, 1977.

Maslow, A. *Motivation and Psychotherapy.* N.Y.: Harper, 1954.

Phillips, E.L. *Psychotherapy: A Modern Theory and Practice.* Englewood Cliffs, N.J.: Prentice-Hall, 1956.

Rogers, C.R., & Dymond, R.F. *Psychotherapy and Personality Change.* Chicago: Univ. of Chicago Press, 1954.

Skinner, B.F. *Beyond Freedom and Human Dignity.* N.Y.: Alfred A. Knopf, 1971.

Skinner, B.F. *Science and Human Behavior.* N.Y.: Macmillan, 1953.

Sloane, R.B., et al. *Psychotherapy Versus Behavior Therapy.* Cambridge: Harvard Univ. Press, 1975.

Wolberg, L.P. *The Technique of Psychotherapy,* 2nd ed. N.Y.: Grune & Stratton, 1967.

Yates, D.H. Relaxation in psychotherapy. *J. Genet. Psychol.,* 1946, *34,* 213-237.

IV. Research and Reports on Psychological Factors in Normal Breast Growth

Baker, J.L., Jr., Kolin, I.S., & Bartlett, E.S. Psychosexual dynamics of patients undergoing mamary augmentation. *Plastic and Reconstructive Surgery,* June, 1974, 652-659.

Brasel, J.A. and Blizzard, R.M., The influence of the endocrine glands upon growth and development. In R.H. Williams (Ed.) *Textbook of Endocrinology.* Phila: W.B. Saunders, 1974.

Brown, B.B., *New Mind, New Body.* N.Y.: Harper and Row, Publishers, 1974.

Coue, E., *Self-Mastery Through Conscious Auto-Suggestion.* London: Allen, 1951.

DeSaxe, B.M., Breast Augmentation. *South African Medical Journal,* 1974, 737-740.

DiCara, L.V., Learning in the Autonomic Nervous System. *Scientific American,* 1970, *222,* 30-39.

Dicker, R.L. and Syracuse, V.R., *Consultation With A Plastic Surgeon.* Chicago: Nelson-Hall Publishers, 1975.

Dunbar, H.F. *Emotions and Bodily Changes,* (4th ed.) N.Y.: Columbia Univ. Press, 1954.

Erickson, M.H., Breast development possibly influenced by hypnosis: Two instances and the therapeutic results. *The American Journal of Clinical Hypnosis,* 1954, *2,* 261-283.

Fisher, S., Aniseikonic perception by women of their own breasts. *Perceptual and Motor Skill,* 1973, *36,* 1021-1022.

Foa, P.P., The Mediation of Psychic Stimuli and Regulation of Endocrine Function. In W.W.Kroger(Ed.),*Psychosomatic Obstetrics, Gynecology and Endocrinology.* Springfield, Ill.: Charles C. Thomas, Publisher, 1962.

Gottschalk, L.A., Self-Induced Visual Imagery, Affect Arousal, and Autonomic Correlates. *Psychosomatics,* 1974, *4,* 166.

Green, E.E., Green, A.M. and Walters, E.D., Self-Regulation of Internal States. *Progress of Cybernetics: Proceedings of the International Congress of Cybernetics.* London Gordon and Breach, 1970, 1299-1317.

Green, E.E., Green, A.M. and Walters, E.D., Voluntary Control of Internal States: Psychological and Physiological. *Journal of Transpersonal Psychology,* 1970, *1,* 1-26.

Hall, H.V., Effects of Direct and Self-Reinforcement as a Function of Internal-External Control. *Perceptual and Motor Skills,* 1973, *37,* 753-754.

Kroger, W.S., *Psychosomatic Obstetrics, Gynecology, and Endocrinology.* Springfield, Ill.: Charles C. Thomas Publisher, 1962.

LeCron, L.M. Breast development through hypnotic suggestion. *Journal of Psychosomatic Dentistry and Medicine,* 1969, *16,* 58-61.

LeCron, L.M. *Self-Hypnotism – The Technique and its Use in Daily Living.* Englewood Cliffs, N.J.: Prentice-Hall, 1964.

Mutke, P.H.C., Self-Image and Breast Development. *Selective Awareness.* Millbrae, CA: Celestial Arts, 1977, 149-156.

Mutke, P.H.C., Research paper on the subject of *Mental Techniques for Breast Development,* presented to the Department of Neuropsychiatry, University of California, Los Angeles, February 28, 1971.

Packard, J. Breast Enlargement with three types of hypnotic suggestions. California State University, at Sacramento, 1979.

Packard, J. *Natural Breast Enlargement Through Effective Relaxation Techniques.* Sacramento, California, Jalmar Press, 1981.

Sihm, F., et al., Psychological Assessment before and after Augmentation Mammaplasty. *Scandanavian Journal of Plastic and Reconstructive Surgery.* 1978, *12,* 295-298.

Staib, A.R. and Logan, D.R., Hypnotic Stimulation of Breast Growth. *The American Journal of Clinical Hypnosis,* 1977, *4,* 201-208.

Vanderhoof, E. and Clancy, J. Effect of Emotion On Blood Flow. *Journal of Applied Physiology,* 1962, *17,* 67.

Willard, R.D. Breast enlargement through visual imagery and hypnosis. *The American Journal of Clinical Hypnosis,* 1977, *4,* 195-200.

Williams, J.E., Stimulation of breast growth by hypnosis. *Journal of Sex Research,* 1974, *10,* 316-326.

Williams, J.E. *Natural Breast Enlargement.* N.Y.: Biogenics Corp., 1979.

Wilson, D.L., *Natural Bust Enlargement with Total Mind Power – How to Use the Other 90% of Your Mind to Increase the Size of Your Breasts.* Larkspur, California: Total Mind Power Institute, 1979.

Wilson, D.L., *Total Beauty Through Total Mind Power – How to Use the Other 90% of Your Mind to Improve Your Beauty.* 1979.

Wilson, D.L., *Total Mind Power – How to Use the Other 90% of Your Mind.* N.Y.: Berkley Publishing Corporation, 1978.

The scientific data presented in this book, and the *New Dimensions Bio-Imagery Programming Figure Enhancement System* discussed in the text, have been prepared under the supervision of an internationally known scientist, and clinical psychologist. A certified Diplomate of the American Board of Professional Psychology, he is the author of widely-used college textbooks and many research articles. He has been a professor of psychology at four leading universities. Voted among the Top Twenty Psychologists who had a significant influence on other psychologists by the American Psychological Association, he is listed in *Who's Who in America,* the the *International Biographies of Notable Men.* He has served as the director of four psychology clinics and as a consultant to national and state agencies, and to hospitals, clinics, and school systems. He serves as Programming Consultant to New Directions, Inc., and critically reviews all Program materials to insure that (1) they accurately reflect the relevant data published in scientific journals, and (2) they conform to present-day scientific knowledge and ethics concerning learning processes, suggestion, imagery, and related scientific procedures.

PROGRESS CHART SURVEY

Your comments about your use of the *New Dimensions* Program can help provide continuing data for our on-going study on its effective use. They can also benefit others interested in using the Program. Please write your comments below, fill in the duplicate Progress Chart on the back of this page, and mail it to: New Directions, Inc., Suite 208, Dept. PCS, 161 Ottawa N.W., Grand Rapids, Michigan 49503.

(Please use additional pages if more space is required)

This gives you my permission to publish the enclosed statements and Progress Chart. I understand that only my initials and city and state will be used with this material.

_____   _____

Signature   Date

New DIMENSIONS® II BIO-IMAGERY PROGRAMMING ™

PROGRESS CHART

NUMBER OF TIMES EACH
PROGRAM WAS USED

MEASUREMENTS
Before starting Program

WEEK Script 1	Script One The Basic Program	Script Two The Accelerated Program	Self-Image Script The Maximum Effects Program	VISUAL-IZATIONS*	BUST	CHEST	WAIST	WEIGHT
1								
2								
3								
4								
Script 1 or 1 and 2								
5								
6								
7								
8								
9								
10								
11								
12								
13								
14								
15								
16								

HOW THE PROGRAM WAS USED
— CHECK ONE (If more than one
method was used, please indicate the
approximate percentage of use for
each method)

☐ READING THE SCRIPTS

☐ REVIEWING THE SCRIPTS
FROM MEMORY

☐ HAVING SOMEONE ELSE
READ THE SCRIPTS TO YOU

☐ LISTENING TO TALKING
BOOK RECORDINGS

NET CHANGE

BUST INCREASE   CHEST DECREASE   WAIST DECREASE   WEIGHT DECREASE

ADD CHEST
DECREASE
TO YOUR
BUST INCREASE   +_____

***TOTAL
BUST INC.

*** Example: If your bust
increases 2 inches and
your chest measurement
immediately below your
breasts decreases 1 inch,
your Total Net Bust In-
crease would be 3 inches.

GOALS

BUST   WAIST   WEIGHT

NAME_____

ADDRESS_____

CITY/STATE/ZIP_____

TALKING BOOK TRANSCRIPTS

ORDER FORM

Talking Book Transcripts — special recordings transcribed from the book — are available for those who prefer this convenience. No medical claims of any sort are made for the recordings (see chapter 7). They are offered only as a convenience for people who enjoy the rapid, effortless, effective ease of learning that recordings can provide. Although the complete Program is in the book, Talking Book Transcripts are especially popular because they can be listened to again and again so easily and effortlessly. They help accelerate and simplify learning and are a marvelous optional addition to the book. A highly effective, useful, and rapid way to learn.

Each recording is available on either 12" LP record or on cassette. Specify your preference on the order form. The recordings are available for $9.95 each. Please add $2.00 to your order for postage and handling.

TALKING BOOK TRANSCRIPTS
ORDER FORM

New Directions, Inc.
Suite 208, Dept. BK-200
161 Ottawa N.W. Grand Rapids, MI 49503

CHECK ONE
☐ 12" LP Record
☐ Cassette

CHECK THE RECORDINGS OF YOUR CHOICE

☐ Chapter 8, *The Basic Program* – Script One $9.95
  (Side 1 – Male Narration
  Side 2 – Female Narration)

☐ Chapter 9, *The Accelerated Program* – Script Two $9.95
  (Side 1 – Male Narration
  Side 2 – Female Narration)

☐ Chapter 14, *The Maximum Effects Program* $9.95
  The Self-Image Script
  (Side 1 – Progressive Relaxation
  Side 2 – Reaching Your Potential)

☐ Special Combination Offer $24.85
  SAVE $5.00 — Includes all 3 Programs
  Shipped in plain wrapper

Enclosed is: ☐ Check ☐ Money Order
CHARGE TO MY: ☐ Visa ☐ Master Charge

_____
Charge Account Number

_____   _____
Exp. Date   Signature

NAME _____

ADDRESS _____

CITY _____

STATE _____ ZIP _____

AMOUNT OF PURCHASE $ _____
Postage & Handling $ _____ $2.00 _____
Mich. residents add
4% State Sales Tax $ _____
Outside USA, add $4.00 $ _____
TOTAL $ _____